Y0-BCT-049

At Issue

Extending the
Human Lifespan

Other Books in the At Issue Series:

At Issue

Extending the Human Lifespan

Tamara Thompson

GREENHAVEN PRESS
A part of Gale, Cengage Learning

GALE
CENGAGE Learning·

Detroit • New York • San Francisco • New Haven, Conn • Waterville, Maine • London

Elizabeth Des Chenes, *Director, Content Strategy*
Cynthia Sanner, *Publisher*
Douglas Dentino, *Manager, New Product*

For more information, contact:
Greenhaven Press
27500 Drake Rd.
Farmington Hills, MI 48331-3535
Or you can visit our Internet site at gale.cengage.com

For product information and technology assistance, contact us at

Gale Customer Support, 1-800-877-4253
For permission to use material from this text or product, submit all requests online at www.cengage.com/permissions

Further permissions questions can be emailed to permissionrequest@cengage.com

Articles in Greenhaven Press anthologies are often edited for length to meet page requirements. In addition, original titles of these works are changed to clearly present the main thesis and to explicitly indicate the author's opinion. Every effort is made to ensure that Greenhaven Press accurately reflects the original intent of the authors. Every effort has been made to trace the owners of copyrighted material.

Cover image © Images.com/Corbis.

LIBRARY OF CONGRESS CATALOGING-IN-PUBLICATION DATA

Extending the human lifespan / Tamara Thompson, book editor.
pages cm. -- (At issue)
Summary: "At Issue: Extending the Human Lifespan: Books in this anthology series focus a wide range of viewpoints onto a single controversial issue, providing in-depth discussions by leading advocates, a quick grounding in the issues, and a challenge to critical thinking skills"—Provided by publisher.
Includes bibliographical references and index.
ISBN 978-0-7377-6836-7 (hardcover) -- ISBN 978-0-7377-6837-4 (paperback)
1. Longevity--Juvenile literature. 2. Medical technology--Moral and ethical aspects--Juvenile literature. 3. Aging--Prevention--Juvenile literature. I. Thompson, Tamara, editor of compilation.
RA776.75.H862 2013
613.2--dc23
2013003074

Printed in the United States of America

-1 0 1 2 3   17 16 15 14 13

Contents

Introduction

The Greek historian Herodotus wrote about its legendary life-extending powers in the fifth century BC. Alexander the Great is said to have journeyed through the Land of Darkness seeking it before he died around 323 BC. Spanish explorer Juan Ponce de León sailed off looking for it and instead discovered Florida in 1513. And from the 1958 Orson Welles film *The Fountain of Youth* to Johnny Depp's 2011 *Pirates of the Caribbean: On Stranger Tides*, popular culture has long been enamored with the quest for the mythical spring said to restore eternal youth to an aging body.

The quest for immortality may figure prominently in myth and legend, but could there really be such a thing as the Water of Life or the Fountain of Youth? Probably not in the literal sense, but modern medicine may offer something similar one day.

The booming field of life-extension science focuses on ways to slow, stop, or reverse the aging process, primarily by using genetic therapies and biomedicine to target the damage that aging does to the body's cells. The premise is that if the cellular changes caused by aging can be halted, older adults will not develop diseases and the aging process could be effectively stopped or even reversed.

Life expectancy in the United States today is 78.6 years, according to the American Human Development Project's 2010–2011 "Measure of America" report, and the maximum natural human lifespan is generally agreed to be less than 130 years. But scientists say those numbers could be just the beginning; some researchers already claim that babies born today in the United States can expect to live to 105 because of all the revolutionary genetic and biomedical advances that are on the horizon.

While most aging researchers agree that routinely extending healthy life by ten or twenty years will soon be within the reach of modern science, others believe that life can be much more dramatically extended—by centuries or perhaps even indefinitely. Genetic modification, artificial organs, therapeutic cloning, tissue regeneration with stem cells, and even nanotechnology to regulate molecular processes and repair cell damage are all promising avenues of research that could possibly lead to radically extended lives within a generation. Using such theoretical treatments, worn-out body parts might be replaced and age-related cell damage that precipitates disease might be routinely repaired. In this radical view of life extension, life could continue indefinitely as long as the body is regularly maintained, much as people maintain antique cars to keep them in running order.

Most biomedical gerontologists, however, take a comparatively more conservative approach, focusing on improving quality of life and achieving longevity gains that are measured in decades rather than centuries. Even so, many experts consider doubling the human lifespan to be eventually feasible, if not inevitable.

In the United States, the first beneficiaries of significant life-extending treatments will likely be members of the baby boom generation, the seventy-six million people born between 1946 and 1964. The boomers are the nation's largest demographic group, and the first members of this massive cohort have already entered their sixties; the last will turn fifty-five in 2019. By 2030, roughly 20 percent of the population will be over sixty-five, compared to less than 13 percent right now. Boomers have long played an influential role in shaping American culture, and they are expected to continue that trend as they age and become the primary consumers of newly emerging life-extension medicines and technologies.

Over the coming decades, boomers will be able to take advantage of incremental advances in biomedicine that could extend their lives, during which time they could then take advantage of further scientific advances, with the hope of someday reaching what radical biogerontologist Aubrey de Grey calls "longevity escape velocity." As explained by Nicholas Agar in his book *Humanity's End*, "The techniques we invent will add years onto the life expectancies of everyone who has access to them. Longevity escape velocity will have arrived when new therapies consistently give us more years than the time it takes to research them."

For those who grow old and die before viable life-extension treatments are available, however, there is already the option of cryopreservation, a procedure in which bodies are preserved for possible future resuscitation by freezing and storing them at minus-196 degrees Fahrenheit, the boiling point of liquid nitrogen. Though there is no existing technology that can reanimate and reverse aging in such a cryonically frozen body, the hope is that future medical science will one day be able to do so. To date, some 250 people have bet on that possibility and been cryopreserved after their deaths, most famously major league baseball player Ted Williams in 2002.

Regardless of what turns out to be possible at the hand of science, even more controversial than the techniques and processes themselves is whether radically extended lifespans would even be desirable or ethical. For many prolongevists (those who advocate the development of life-extension technologies), extending life is a moral imperative, and they argue that science has an ethical duty to extend the human lifespan as far as possible.

Critics of life extension, however, argue that any dramatic gain in life expectancy could have far-reaching and devastating consequences. They warn of profound demographic shifts as the old make up an ever larger percentage of the population; resource scarcity as demand grows for limited global supplies of water, food, and energy; social strain between generations as they navigate redefined social structures; economic strife as the old compete with the young for jobs throughout their longer working lives; health care inequality as the rich are able to afford life extension medicine and the poor cannot; political entrenchment as the tenure of world leaders lengthens along with their lifespans; and even psychological and spiritual distress as people grapple with new questions of purpose, destiny, and fulfillment as they live to unprecedented ages.

The authors in *At Issue: Extending the Human Lifespan* represent a wide range of viewpoints concerning the ethics, practicalities and consequences of using science to radically extend human life.

1

Radical Life Extension: An Overview

George Dvorsky

George Dvorsky is chairman of the Institute for Ethics and Emerging Technologies, a nonprofit think tank founded in 2004 by philosopher Nick Bostrom and bioethicist James Hughes. The organization's mission is to be a center for voices arguing for a responsible, constructive, and ethical approach to the world's most powerful emerging technologies, including radical life extension science.

There are several types of arguments that typically come up when people talk about the possibilities of human life extension. Those who oppose life extension generally base their arguments on one or more of the following: the appeal to nature, undesirable psychological consequences, negative social consequences, the idea that questionable attitudes and skewed priorities motivate those who desire life extension, and basic fallacies and ad hominem attacks. Proponents of life extension, on the other hand, tend to center their arguments on moral and legal issues, positive social consequences, emphasizing the value of life and the undesirability of death, and recognizing that medical science will inevitably increase the human lifespan—regardless of the debate about the desirability and consequences of doing so. Understanding the arguments put forth by each side allows for a more thoughtful dialogue on this important topic.

I am speaking today about the most popular arguments for and against longevity. This is not going to be a discussion of the scientific arguments that are put forth—I will leave that to the biogerontologists and the specialists. These are the kind of arguments that do come out of academia and some of the political lobbies, but these are also the kind of arguments you hear from the person on the street that you bump into. If you mention this in casual conversation, you can almost assuredly expect these kinds of retorts and objections to these sorts of issues of life extension. So this is to arm ourselves and to think about the various ideas that are out there. . . .

Again, these are not necessarily the best arguments. By no means are these the most valid or credible arguments. It's simply a discussion of what's out there in terms of the discussions that are happening today. I'm not going to be analyzing the arguments for their worth. . . .

The appeal to nature essentially states that meaning to life is somehow something that you pull out of your mortality.

Sources of Opposition

We are going to start off with the opposition to radical life extension. I discovered that there tends to be three main sources opponents will draw their main arguments from. There tend to be the moral and the ethical arguments. There are the practical arguments, which are the real hard-and-fast inhibitors to life extension, where they may not have an ethical problem with it, but they say we cannot do it, because there are fallacies built in. Because I found so many of them, I thought I should probably include them.

Here is what I came up with. There were five broad categories in which I hope you could pigeonhole any argument you can find in opposition to radical life extension:

- The appeal to nature
- Undesirable psychological consequences
- Undesirable social consequences
- The desire for life extension comes from questionable ambitions and skewed priorities
- Fallacies used to argue against life extension

The Appeal to Nature

One of the most common arguments that is put forth in opposition to life extension is the appeal to nature. I'm sure we are all familiar with this—the suggestion that what is natural is inherently good or right, and that what is unnatural is somehow bad or wrong.

A number of critics make the claim that life extension is a violation of the natural order—that humanity is tampering with nature, which is inherently good. It's often argued that the quest for life extension goes against the natural cycles of birth and death, and if we attain immortality we will have stepped so far outside the natural order that we could no longer be considered as humans. Advocates of this view believe that life extension is a dehumanizing usurpation of the natural order. Some of the most outspoken proponents of this view include Leon Kass, Francis Fukuyama, Bill McKibben, and Daniel Callahan. For them, death is seen as something that is very much in our collective and personal best interest, which would run into direct contradiction to what the life extensionists argue.

McKibben, for example, argues that without death, life would be robbed of its meaning. Humans would not have the opportunity to sacrifice for their children. There would be no reason to pour out a life's worth of work out under the literal deadline of mortality. This adjunct in the appeal to nature essentially states that meaning to life is somehow something that you pull out of your mortality—a limited lifespan motivates people to spend their time wisely, and it is through a sense of urgency, they argue, that we are able to refine and exploit our best qualities. Even things like courage, heroism, sacrifice, and creativity arise from the acknowledgment that I and everyone else only has so much time here. Consequently, the implication is that life extension would create a population that is lazy, spoiled, apathetic, self-centered and indulgent, and that life would not be serious or meaningful without death.

The Need for Morality

Death, apparently, also provides us with morality and a need for morality. We could not and would not sacrifice ourselves for something if we were immortal. In this sense, attributes such as virtue and morality have a direct relationship with our condition as vulnerable, transient entities and in how we suffer and sacrifice. Death, therefore, has a social function in this regard. Self-sacrifice, dying in combat or policing, so-called honorable deaths, are part of the normal social functioning of society.

Another argument against life extension is the idea that it would cause people to become extremely conservative and risk-averse. Who wants to risk their indefinite lifespan to go hang gliding or parachute jumping, and so forth? I guess the argument here is that if you are only going to live to be about 80 years-old, it's not so much that I'm putting at risk. But if it's a thousand years, or 10,000 years, suddenly the stakes are much higher. The fear is that you would have a very conservative, risk-averse society that would not have any fun. It's also been argued by such thinkers as Leon Kass that not only would life be devoid of meaning, but beauty is derived by both the object's and the subject's impermanence in the world. Quoting Kass, "Just as a pretty flower is beautiful because we know it will eventually wilt, the sunset is beautiful because it is short-lived."

Utopian Ideals

The anti-life extension camp is also very sensitive to what might be called utopian ideals. They often champion imperfections of humanity. Bill McKibben, the author of *Enough: Staying Human in an Engineered Age* writes, "I like this body and all its limitations, up to and including the fact that it's going to die." A key element of the call to nature argument is in fact its human-centeredness. Life extension interventions are condemned in the same way that transhumanist technologies are condemned, whether they be genetic modifications or cybernetic enhancements—that these are interventions that will somehow dehumanize us or lessen what we currently are. Again, quoting from Kass, "The pursuit of perfect bodies and further life extension will deflect us from realizing more fully the aspirations to which our lives naturally point: for living well, rather than merely staying alive."

The passion of youth is a commonly cited argument against life extension.

As a subset to the call to nature there perhaps is the call to the unnatural—nonsecular variations of the naturalistic appeal. That is, there are broader metaphysical implications to death—that the materialist assumption is wrong and something does in fact await us on the other side. Heaven, some kind of transcendental rebirth, or what have you. I have heard that from time to time.

Psychological Consequences

The inadequacy of the human psyche to deal with radical longevity. It is a distinctive argument, but there is considerable cross-over between this line of thinking and the line of argumentation that was just put forward. That humans would be bored, apathetic, and so on—these are assertions that human psychology is not set up to deal with. It is distinctive, however, from the naturalist argument in that this is named as a practical barrier to life extension, rather than the more abstract call for the preservation of the natural and the moral delineation between good and bad.

This is the big one. We're going to be bored when we have indefinite lifespans. We would be bored and life would be full of repetitious tedium. So severe would this boredom be actually that we should probably forgo life extension altogether. It is an unpredictable social experiment—we do not know what will await us beyond our expected normal lifespan right now. It is dangerous and reckless for us to go down that path. As [singer-songwriter] John Cougar Mellencamp once said, "Life goes on long after the thrill of living is gone." Indeed, the passion of youth is a commonly cited argument against life extension.

But as Mark Walker noted in a paper called "Boredom, Experimental Ethics, and Superlongevity," boredom seems like a rather trivial objection to radical life extension. Really what is being discussed is a bit more profound and deep-rooted, and that is the condition of *ennui*. The condition of ennui is a state of chronic and debilitating apathy and disdain. "Ennui" is derived from the Greek term 'to be annoyed.' It is defined as a reactive state to wearyingly dull, repetitive or tedious stimuli, suffering from a lack of interesting things to see or do. It is a condition of pervasive boredom, in the sense that one tires of the earth itself. And the only solution, as some philosophers have posited, such as Bernard Williams, is death.

Madness and Self-Continuity

There is also the possibility of madness—that we would go insane for having such long lives. Take for example the *Twilight Zone* episode "A Nice Place to Visit," in which a gambler who believes himself to be in heaven is in a casino and he is winning all the tables. He cannot possibly lose, and he's loving this at first, but as time goes by it's starting to get a little predictable, it gets boring and then it gets tedious. It gets so bad for him that he actually at this point wishes to be sent to the "other place." At which point, we have our classic *Twilight Zone* ending narration: a scared, angry little man who never got a break. Now he has everything he's ever wanted and he's going to have to live with it for an eternity in the Twilight Zone.

This is an interesting one: that we will lose a sense of psychological self-continuity over time. I know that as someone who is 30-something, I can certainly relate to this. I do remember what it was like to be in my early 20's, and even as a teenager, but I am so far removed from that person as to be a different person altogether. The suggestion is that given hundreds of years, if not thousands of years, that you will be so detached from your previous self, so detached from the person who bought into life extension, that it actually defeats the purpose of life extension, because the person who wanted life extension no longer exists. This is the argument—I'm not saying it's a great argument.

Not only might there be psychological consequences to life extension but severe and intractible social consequences.

Social Consequences

In principle, one could be in favor of life extension on moral grounds, but be opposed to it due to the practical applications of its onset. Not only might there be psychological consequences to life extension but severe and intractible social consequences, such as the so-called Tragedy of the Commons [wherein individuals deplete a shared common resource in their own self-interest, to the detriment of the entire group]. . . .

There are of course the issues of social and distributive injustices. Life extension interventions, it is argued, are bound to be both cost prohibitive to a large segment of the population, and I guess the assumption is that the widening gap between the rich and poor will lead to greater social inequality.

Demographic Effects

Another undesirable social consequence is undesirable demographic skews. If only the rich have access, for example, both racial and class balances might be upset, and will end up in a divided world with parallel populations and new classes altogether. Francis Fukuyama has warned that we risk creating a "nursing home world" filled with aging, miserable, debilitated people draining resources from the young to keep themselves alive. More realistically to what we are addressing, in a world where elderly people would remain forever physically and psychologically vibrant, workplace demographics and the issue of retirement would become pertinent. How will younger generations work their way into positions of more authority if the older generation never has to give up those roles? This is what legal philosopher Steven Horrobin has called "The Problem of Incumbency." In a world of life extension, people of authority, wealth, or power would remain there indefinitely. There could be the problem of generational dominance. Misguided and deviant people would not wither away and die. Elites would not give up their positions, either in business or in politics.

Malthusian Scenarios

There is also the threat of scientific and cultural stagnation. It is a well-known cycle of life, it has been argued, and it may provide other benefits to society—the elimination of death may curtail the important social processes that we take for granted. There is the possibility that there would be fewer fresh ideas. Quantum physicist Max Planck once said, "A new scientific truth does not triumph by convincing its opponents and making them see the light, but rather because its opponents eventually die, and a new generation grows up that is familiar with it." Similarly in the context of social change, the issue of same-sex marriages is culturally divided almost exclusively along demographic lines, where you have an older generation that is very uneasy about it and a younger generation for which it is an absolute no-brainer. So this kind of thing could result in cultural and social stagnation.

Issues of overpopulation, environmental non-sustainabillty, and other Malthusian scenarios are extremely common arguments levied against the concept of radical life extension. Environmentalist E.O. Wilson has calculated that for every person in the world to reach present U.S. levels of consumption with existing technology, you would need four planet earths. Suffice to say, life extension would greatly compound the issue. This is very much a neo-Malthusian argument. In terms of the earth's food, water, and energy, everything that makes up our global footprint, cannot possibly keep up with a perpetually increasing population.

Questionable Motivations and Skewed Priorities

Opponents of life extension frequently question the motivations of those in search of extended lives and suggest that there are much more pressing concerns for human civilization. A number of critics like Callahan believe that our motivations for wanting extended lives is deeply problematic, and there is no known social good coming from the conquest of death. The quest for life extension has been referred to as "antisocial," and those who wish to live longer lives have been called selfish, arrogant, hubristic, irreverent, childish, and narcissistic . . . and those are the nice things they have to say about life extensionists. Critics are also aware of the potential for life extension to hit the mainstream. Consequently, some critics have already made the proclamation that governments should be required to intervene and do what is right for society, because people will not do what is in society's collective best interest. The state will be required to uphold the social good.

Everyone is familiar with ad hominem attacks against life extensionists.

Brian Alexander, who authored the book *Rapture: How Biotechnology Became the New Religion*, once asked Francis Fukuyama if the government has the right to tell its citizens if they have to die, and Fukuyama answered, "Yes. Absolutely." Leon Kass has noted, "The finitude of human life is a blessing for every individual, whether he knows it or not." John Harris, author of *Immortal Ethics* has referred to this threat, I suppose, as "generational cleansing." At some point, because the technologies actually exist, that this would be a kind of genocide enforced upon the elderly population. The idea is that some cleansing will have to be enacted in the interest of society.

Again from Kass, "Simply to covet a prolonged lifespan for ourselves is both a sign and a cause of our failure to open ourselves to procreation and to any higher purpose. The desire to prolong youthfulness is not only a childish desire to eat one's life and keep it, but it is also an expression of a childish and narcissistic wish incompatible with the devotion to posterity." Again, there is something wrong with life extensionists and their quest for long life. Furthermore, there are more important problems to be dealing with right now: global warming, human poverty, disease.

Logical Fallacies

Now, arguably life extension has been the target at times of pseudo-skepticism, which is characterized by unfair, biased, presupposed and overzealous lines of attack. Everyone is familiar with ad hominem attacks against life extensionists.

They are characterized as being pseudo-scientists or practicioners of pathological science. Again, I think this speaks to the high degree of emotionalism that is invested in the issue.

The suggestion is that there is something deeply wrong with life extensionists. A couple years ago, *Technology Review*'s Editor in Chief Jason Pontin laid into Aubrey de Grey, using the opportunity not so much to critique "Strategies for Engineered Negligible Senescence" but to launch personal attacks, referring to Aubrey, forgive me, as a "troll." He slammed Aubrey as a person, questioned his life choices, and criticized his personal habits and appearance. We're not talking about man on the street, this is the editor of *Technology Review* magazine.

Nor does it have to be a character attack like this. It can also be an accusation of psychological instability, "quirkiness," or eccentricity. *Psychology Today* recently put out an article about life extensionist Michael Anissimov called "Champions of the Lost Cause." The presence of the piece in a psychology magazine, even if it might be a popular magazine, hinted that Anissimov's quest for life extension was somehow psychologically quirky or eccentric, not something a normal person would want to pursue for themselves.

Arguments for Longevity

For those of us who are in promotion of life extension, we also will put forward ethical reasons and practical arguments for doing so, although it's very top-heavy in the first category.

Life is good, death is bad. That pretty much says it all for life extensionists.

To date, the arguments have been almost exclusively about why life is valuable, not really having the evidence or wherewithal to develop some hard-and-fast reasons from a social or economic perspective as to why we should do this. This is why an event like this is so unbelievably encouraging. One can make the case now that it's starting to happen, we are putting forth arguments for the social and economic benefits of life extension. I find that arguments on behalf [of] life extension tend to be somewhat on the offensive. We are under attack and many of the arguments are meant to deflect criticism.

There are four broad categories to the arguments of pro-longevists: the value of life and undesirability of death, the ethical and legal right to life extension, that there are desirable social consequences, and that it is an issue more of working toward the inevitable than striving toward the feasible.

Life is good, death is bad. That pretty much says it all for life extensionists. But that being said, you can't just say, "Life is good." It's almost a self-evidentiary argument. We have to at least justify why it is the act of living that we value, not just "life" itself.

There is the notion that death at the age of 17 is far more tragic than death at the age of 87. The life extensionists would respond that this is based on our conditioned response and expectations of a maximum lifespan. If we could live to 1000, therefore would we consider the death of someone at 350 to be just as tragic? Is this an issue of relativity? Could we ever come up with a maximum lifespan that is not arbitrary? I argue, absolutely not.

Existential Questions

These issues, they do have deep existential connotations. There is a panoply of related issues, including the meaning of a good life, the infinite totality that is death, and the bizarre acknowledgment that we exist in the first place.

It was said by the Greek philosopher Epicurus that death is nothing to us when we are dead. Death is a non-condition. That said, death is most certainly to the frustration of the living. People who desire to go on living, they have objectives for the future, objectives which it is hoped will translate into real experiences. Death can be seen as the denier of these desires, which is why death is seen as something that is so undesirable

A great quote from [writer] J.R.R. Tolkien: "There is no such thing as a natural death. Nothing that happens to Man is ever natural, since his presence calls the whole world into question. All men must die, but for every man his death is an accident. And even if he knows it and consents to it, an unjustifiable violation." I love how that is almost an absolute obverse to Leon Kass's issue about how death is valuable whether we know it or not. Tolkien argued that it is unjustifiable whether we know it or not.

Not only might there be psychological consequences to life extension but severe and intractible social consequences.

Again, death tends to be seen as something overwhelmingly undesirable and wasteful—accumulated memories, experiences and the wisdom of others has been lost forever upon death. Moreover, it is a terrible thing for us to have to deal with death. Quoting Eliezer Yudkowsky, who experienced the death of a sibling a few years ago, "death is nothing any sentient being should have to deal with."

Life extensionists are cognizant of the fact that hundreds of thousands of people die each day. They have a death counter in mind. This is how they do frame it, as a kind of global catastrophe, and therefore it does extend into a civil rights issue—that it is among our rights as individuals to manipulate and transform our bodies as we see fit.

Socioeconomic Disparities

Because so many of the opponents to life extension have argued that we should eliminate it altogether because not everyone can immediately have access to it, the pro-longevists would say that this does not make it therefore unjust to develop life extension anyway for those who can initially afford it. In denying affluent groups the right to life extension out of consideration for the societal divides, John Davis has said that in other contexts we accept the general principle—that taking from the haves is only justified when it makes the have-nots more than marginally better off. If life extension is possible, one must waive the light fears at stake for those who receive the treatment against whatever burdens making such treatments available might impose on the have-nots who cannot afford the treatments. Again, one thing that the IEET [Institute for Ethics and Emerging Technologies] is very cognizant of is working to ensure that these types of technologies have as broad access as possible.

Preventing the development and proliferation of life extending technologies would be extremely difficult and dangerous.

Positive Social Consequences

The potential for long lives, say the pro-longevists, will have positive social consequences. It has been said that one consequence of a protracted life is increased personal responsibility and accountability. Individuals would have a longer time to deal with the repercussions of their negative actions. Long lived people will have developed a deep and profound wisdom, particularly as pertains to social relationships. Nick Bostrom has argued that with longer life expectancy, people will have a personal stake in the future, and this will lead to more responsibility and sustainable policies. It also makes utilitarians happy. Michael Anissimov has said that life extension is important to utilitarians because billions of people want it. Utilitarianism is about doing what makes people happy, so life extension is automatically a utilitarian priority.

Another interesting take, one I am somewhat partial to, is that we're actually talking about, as James would say, arguing against the plow. Let's talk about how we are going to manage the process and get into the whole issue of obligations. Again, this is one argument made on behalf of life extension. We all know what life expectancy and health habits have done over the past one hundred years. To this end, we should be arguing for the conquest of disease, to give seniors a higher quality of physical lives.

The Transhumanist Argument

Transhumanists and humanists in general would argue that this is the continuation of the human mission in general. Combined with the legal and ethical aspect, we have to bring this within the purview of responsibilities as compassionate people.

Injunctions against the development of life extension would most assuredly open up a Pandora's box of problems. Preventing the development and proliferation of life extending technologies would be extremely difficult and dangerous. Demand would be through the roof, with desperate people willing to do virtually anything to get their hands on these things. It could cause a number of problems, including black markets, unregulated labs and testing.

If we can actually show that the seemingly practical inhibitors to life extension are surmountable, in what ways are we now obligated to do these things? Aubrey de Grey has argued that we are responsible to future generations. *Reason*'s science correspondent Ronald Bailey has noted that our ancestors, our grandparents and parents, did not ask our permission to do so—they just went ahead and did it. It is unlikely that our descendants will have any more reason to regret our decisions than we have to regret our forbears'.

A number of technologists contend that many of the opponents of life extension ignore the advancements that are happening, that we may drastically reduce the global foot-print, resolve environmental problems, harness safe alternative high-energy sources, learn to manage the potential physiological and psychological artifacts of life extension, even alternative living arrangements that could house millions of people, and so on. Quoting [inventor and futurist] Ray Kurzweil, "We need to expand our intelligence and our capacity for experience, which is exactly what new technologies will enable us to do. Then an extended lifespan would become not only tolerable but a remarkable frontier where we could pursue the real purpose of life."

2

Aging Is a Disease That Science Should Cure

David Gems

David Gems is deputy director of the Institute of Healthy Ageing at University College London. He leads a research team that uses model organisms to understand the biology of aging and search for ways to improve late-life health and wellbeing.

Many people who oppose life extension science do so because they believe the physical decline associated with aging (known as senescence) is a natural part of life and that senescence itself is not a disease. Research in the field of biogerontology—the biology of aging—shows a very different conclusion, however. Because the molecular, cellular, and physiological declines of senescence happen long after a person is past their reproductive years, those maladaptive late-life traits have been allowed to pass from generation to generation over the centuries. Instead of being reduced or phased out through natural selection, as would happen with negative traits that affect young individuals, the elderly have already successfully reproduced before their senescence can be selected out of the gene pool. This means that aging is actually a multifactor genetic disease; science must pursue the ethical course and seek a way to decelerate the late-life disease process.

The 20th century brought both profound suffering and profound relief to people around the world. On the one hand, it produced political lunacy, war and mass murder on

David Gems, "Aging: To Treat, or Not to Treat? The Possibility of Treating Aging Is Not Just an Idle Fantasy," *American Scientist*, vol. 99, no. 4, July–August 2011, pp. 278–280.

an unprecedented scale. But there were also extraordinary gains—not least in public health, medicine and food production. In the developed world, we no longer live in constant fear of infectious disease. Furthermore, a Malthusian catastrophe of global population growth exceeding food production—a terrifying prospect predicted first in the 18th century—did not materialize. This is largely due to a steep decline in birth rates, for which we can thank the education, emancipation and rationality of women. Most people in the developed world can now expect to live long lives.

Yet, as too often happens, the solution of one problem spawns others. Because we are having fewer children and living longer, the developed world is now filling up with old people. In Japan, for example, where the population is aging particularly quickly, the ratio of people less than 20 years old to those over 65 is plummeting, from 9.3 in 1950 to a predicted 0.59 in 2025. In Europe and the United States, we see ever more bald and grey heads on streets and in parks and shopping malls. Although this is something to celebrate, old age unfortunately has myriad ways of making us ill. It brings cardiovascular disease that leads to heart attacks and strokes; neurodegenerative diseases such as Alzheimer's and Parkinson's that erode the self; and macular degeneration, which blinds. And, of course, there is cancer. Aging has been described as the greatest of all carcinogens. Like the pandemic of obesity, the increasing number of people living long enough to experience these illnesses is, in some ways, a side effect of progress. Now we face this challenging question: Should we attack the underlying cause of this suffering? Should we try to "cure" aging?

I am a scientist working in the growing field of biogerontology—the biology of aging. The cause of aging remains one of the great unsolved scientific mysteries. Still, the past decade has brought real progress in our understanding, raising the prospect that treatments might one day be feasible. Yet aging is not just another disease. And the prospect of treating aging is extraordinary in terms of the potential impact on the human condition. So, would it be ethical to try to treat it?

In evolutionary terms, aging appears to serve no real purpose, meaning it does not contribute to evolutionary fitness.

Is Aging a Disease?

One argument against treating aging is that it is not a disease. To an extent, this view stems from the fact that the word aging refers to different things. One is the experience of the passage of time. Another is the acquisition of experience and wisdom that can come from living long. To avoid confusion with these benign aspects, biologists use the term "senescence" for the increasing frailty and risk of disease and death that come with aging. Put more precisely, then, the question at hand is this: Is human senescence a disease?

One approach to defining illness has been to compare a given condition to good health. Is someone's condition typical of a person of a given gender or age? For instance, the possession of ovaries is healthy for a woman, but not a man. Likewise, one might consider muscle wasting to indicate serious disease in a 20-year-old, but not a 90-year-old. Given that everyone who lives long enough will eventually experience senescence, I can appreciate the view that it is a normal condition and therefore not pathological. Still, from my perspective as someone working on the biological basis of aging, it is hard not to see it as a disease.

Senescence is a process involving dysfunction and deterioration at the molecular, cellular and physiological levels. This endemic malfunction causes diseases of aging. Even if one ages well, escaping the ravages of cancer or type II diabetes, one still dies in the end, and one dies of something. Moreover, in evolutionary terms, aging appears to serve no real purpose, meaning it does not contribute to evolutionary fitness. Why, then, has aging evolved? The main theory dates back to the 1930s and was developed by J.B.S. Haldane and, later, Peter Medawar—both of University College London—and by the American biologist George C. Williams of the State University of New York, Stony Brook. It argues that aging reflects the decline in the force of natural selection against mutations that exert harmful effects late in life. An inherited mutation causing severe pathology in childhood will reduce the chances of reproduction and so disappear from the population. By contrast, another mutation with similar effects—but which surfaces after a person's reproductive years—is more likely to persist. Natural selection can even favor mutations that enhance fitness early in life but reduce late-life health. This is because the early-life effects of genes have much stronger effects on fitness. Consequently, populations accumulate mutations that exert harmful effects in late life, and the sum of these effects is aging. Here evolutionary biology delivers a grim message about the human condition: Aging is essentially a multifactor genetic disease. It differs from other genetic diseases only in that we all inherit it. This universality does not mean that aging is not a disease. Instead, it is a special sort of disease.

A New Ethical Imperative

A different worry about redefining aging as a disease is that it would lead to stigmatization of the elderly. Perhaps, but the recognition of late-onset Alzheimer's disease as a pathology created an ethical imperative for research to understand and treat the condition. One might expect the same to be true of aging. Such a redefinition would also help to counter the blight that is the wholesale swindling of the elderly by practitioners of so-called anti-aging medicine. In the United States, the Food and Drug Administration (FDA) assures the safety and efficacy of medical treatments. Yet because aging is not viewed as a disease, orally administered drugs marketed as treatments for aging (resveratrol, for example) are subject only to the much laxer FDA regulations that apply to dietary supplements. Redefining aging as a disease would not only energize research into treatments, it would shut down the snake-oil peddlers.

The realization that aging can be manipulated has profound implications for people.

The possibility of treating aging is not just an idle fantasy. One of the most remarkable discoveries in biology in recent decades is one that surprisingly few people know about: It is possible to slow aging in laboratory animals. In fact, it is easy. Work in my own lab focuses on the tiny nematode worm *Caenorhabditis elegans*, which is widely used in genetic studies. Even under optimal culture conditions, these creatures age and die within two to three weeks. In the early 1980s the American geneticist Michael Klass first discovered that by altering their genes, one can slow aging in *C. elegans*. The result is that the worms live much longer and they remain youthful and healthy longer. The current record for enhancing *C. elegans* longevity is an astonishing tenfold increase in lifespan, produced by a group at the University of Arkansas. It has now been shown that genes that influence aging in the worms also influence aging in mammals (in mice, to be precise). Humans also carry these genes.

By identifying genes that control aging rates, we can also learn about the underlying biology of aging. We can explore the aging-related processes that the genes influence. Many aging genes are associated with a nutrient-sensitive signalling network that includes insulinlike growth factor 1 (IGF-1) and an intracellular protein called TOR. Dampening the signals that this network transmits slows growth, increases resistance to stress and increases lifespan. Work in my laboratory and others at the Institute of Healthy Ageing in University College London aims to understand how exactly this network works to control aging. Answering this involves addressing the big question: What produces aging? One theory attributes it to an accumulation of molecular damage. Another points to excess biosynthesis; many genes and pathways that influence aging are associated with control of biosynthesis and growth. Yet the truth remains unclear.

Why One Threat at a Time?

The realization that aging can be manipulated has profound implications for people. Controlled reduction of food intake (dietary restriction) can improve late-life health and increase lifespan in mammals, from rodents to rhesus monkeys. Whether it might do the same in humans is currently under investigation. One aim of aging research is to develop drugs that can reproduce the effects of dietary restriction and also of genetic alterations that slow aging. One approach could be to use drug therapy to target the nutrient-sensitive pathways that regulate aging (for example, TOR) and that seem to mediate the effects of dietary restriction on aging. The ultimate goal would be a pill that one could take regularly from midlife onward. This pill would theoretically slow aging with minimal side effects. Its predicted impact would be to reduce the incidence of aging-related disease at all ages—although not to remove them altogether. This would lengthen good health later into life and extend our lifespan—possibly without expanding periods of disability and dependency.

Such an approach could revolutionize the ways that diseases of aging are combated. Currently they are, by and large, tackled individually. One scientist studies heart disease, another Alzheimer's disease, another macular degeneration and so on. Yet such ailments are symptoms of a larger underlying syndrome: aging. It is for this reason that there is a law of diminishing returns when it comes to treating diseases of aging.

The battle with aging is akin to that between Heracles, the hero of Greek mythology, and the multiheaded Hydra. Each time Heracles hacked off a head, two more would sprout in its place. Likewise, the old man successfully treated for prostate cancer may not long afterward stagger back into the physician's office with macular degeneration and dementia. Such piecemeal approaches to treating age-related illness have undoubtedly improved late-life health to an extent and they have increased life expectancy. This, again, is something to celebrate. Yet in the long run a more powerful way to protect against age-related disease would be to intervene in the aging process itself. This would provide protection against the full spectrum of age-related illnesses. Returning to our classical illustration, to really defeat the diseases of late life we need to strike at the heart of the Hydra of senescence: the aging process itself. But is this actually where biogerontology is headed?

No Concensus on Biogerontology

After establishing my own research laboratory some years ago, I found myself brooding about the purpose of biogerontology. As a scientist working on aging, what exactly should I be trying to achieve? What was the big plan? I began asking other biogerontologists and soon discovered that there was no unified vision regarding what to do about aging once we understood it. I realized that I'd have to try to figure this out for myself. It helped that a few people had wondered about this before, particularly in medical ethics. In 2003 Eric Juengst at Case Western Reserve University identified three distinct goals for biogerontology. One he called *compressed morbidity*. This entails improving late-life health while avoiding any major extension of lifespan. Another was *arrested aging*, that is to say, stopping aging altogether. And the third was *decelerated aging*, slowing down the aging process. Putting aside the question of the pros and cons of each goal, only decelerated aging seemed plausible to me, given recent developments in biogerontology.

But is this a type of medicine that humanity should pursue? As I see it, decelerating human aging would have two outcomes in ethical terms. On the one hand, it would reduce disease on an enormous scale. This would be a great good. On the other hand, it would lead to life extension, perhaps eventually of a large magnitude. This second outcome is controversial. Surveys of public opinion, for example by researchers at the University of Queensland in Australia in 2009, suggest that most people would favor this outcome, but not all. There have been some vocal opponents. Yet, given the great benefit of decelerated aging in terms of reduced suffering, I feel we must pursue this approach, despite the misgivings.

The fact is that no medical treatment reduces a person's overall risk of dying.

New Ethical Challenges

Although decelerated aging seems a goal that should be pursued, it still has some troubling features. One relates to a question that I sometimes get asked about mice whose life has been extended: What do they die of? The answer is a range of aging-related illnesses, similar to those afflicting the untreated mice. But if the mice still die from aging-related diseases, people ask, what is the benefit? All that has been achieved is that the diseases have been delayed for a while. It is quite true that decelerated aging is not predicted to reduce lifelong risk of terminal disease. Yet one has to put this into perspective. The fact is that no medical treatment reduces a person's overall risk of dying. For example, it is logical to assume that the development of a cure for tuberculosis led to an increase in the frequency of Alzheimer's disease. It must have since it raised the proportion of people living to ripe old ages, when the erasing hand of Alzheimer's strikes. Sadly, the probability that each of us will die as the result of some severe pathology is 100 percent, and this can never change. So it goes, as [writer] Kurt Vonnegut, Jr., used to say. Ultimately, the success of any medical treatment should be gauged in terms of the degree to which it extends a healthy lifespan. Viewed against such a moral yardstick, one can see that decelerated aging would be of great benefit.

Measuring Success

Here's another worry, though. I argue for the recognition of an imperative to seek treatments that decelerate aging in order to alleviate late-life diseases. But at what point would such an imperative be fulfilled? Although decelerating aging would postpone the illnesses of aging, it would not make them any less awful. This means that achieving decelerated aging would not lessen the imperative. We would only be compelled to decelerate aging further, and then further still. Here the ethical calculus seems to set us inexorably on a road to ever-greater life extension. Could any sane authority ever opt to force others to forego treatment and suffer from avoidable age-related disease? Surely not.

So it is that decelerated aging would force a dilemma upon us. Should we alleviate suffering on a large scale and accept life extension? Or should we allow an immensity of avoidable suffering in order to avoid extending life? To my mind, the only reasonable course is the first. In fact, we should pursue it energetically, and begin to prevent illness as soon as is feasible. If not, we risk the fury of future generations for dithering. As for life extension, we will just have to take that on the chin. If we can prepare for it socially, politically and institutionally, and if we keep birth rates low, we should be able to ensure long, healthier, happier lives for our children and for our children's children.

3

Radical Life Extension Raises Complex Social, Economic, and Political Issues

Bennett Foddy, interviewed by Ross Andersen

Bennett Foddy is a philosopher from Oxford who has written extensively about the ethics of life extension. Ross Andersen is a Washington, DC-based correspondent for The Atlantic. *He is also the science editor at the* Los Angeles Review of Books *and a contributor to* The Economist.

Human life extension is not a futuristic concept. In fact, the human lifespan has been doubled from forty to eighty years over just a few generations, thanks to advances in medical science and modern sanitation practices. So it should not seem strange that the typical human lifespan could soon be doubled again. Currently available medical interventions allow individuals to live more years in declining health, which creates a big strain on society both economically and socially. Globally, there is already a longevity wealth gap—a disparity between the rich and poor as far as who has access to health care and life-extending treatments, and who does not. These issues will become even more important as treatments are developed to extend the lifespan even more dramatically over the coming decades.

So far as we know, the last hundred years have been the most radical period of life extension in all of human history. At the turn of the twentieth century, life expectancy for

Americans was just over 49 years; by 2010, that number had risen to 78.5 years, mostly on account of improved sanitation and basic medicine. But life extension doesn't always increase our well-being, especially when all that's being extended is decrepitude. There's a reason that [sixteenth-century Spanish explorer] Ponce de Leon went searching for the fountain of youth—if it were the fountain of prolonged dementia and arthritis he may not have bothered.

Over the past twenty years, biologists have begun to set their sights on the aging process itself, in part by paying close attention to species like the American Lobster, which, despite living as long as fifty years, doesn't seem to age much at all. Though some of this research has shown promise, it's not as though we're on the brink of developing a magical youth potion. Because aging is so biologically complex, encompassing hundreds of different processes, it's unlikely that any one technique will add decades of youth to our lives. Rather, the best we can hope for is a slow, incremental lengthening of our "youth-span," the alert and active period of our lives.

Not everyone is thrilled by the prospect of radical life extension. As funding for anti-aging research has exploded, bioethicists have expressed alarm, reasoning that extreme longevity could have disastrous social effects. Some argue that longer life spans will mean stiffer competition for resources, or a wider gap between rich and poor. Others insist that the aging process is important because it gives death a kind of time release effect, which eases us into accepting it. These concerns are well founded. Life spans of several hundred years are bound to be socially disruptive in one way or another; if we're headed in that direction, it's best to start teasing out the difficulties now.

Evolutionary Arguments

But there is another, deeper argument against life extension—the argument from evolution. Its proponents suggest that we ought to avoid tinkering with *any* human trait borne of natural selection. Doing so, they argue, could have unforeseen consequences, especially given that natural selection has such a sterling engineering track record. If our bodies grow old and die, the thinking goes, then there must be a good reason, even if we don't understand it yet. Nonsense, says Bennett Foddy, a philosopher from Oxford, who has written extensively about the ethics of life extension. "We think about aging as being a natural human trait, and it is natural, but it's not something that was selected for because it was beneficial to us," Foddy told me. "There is this misconception that everything evolution provides is beneficial to individuals and that's not correct."

There's always this background moral objection in enhancement debates, where a technology is perceived to be new, and by virtue of being new, is depicted as threatening or even strange.

Foddy has thought long and hard about the various objections to life extension and, for the most part, has found them wanting. This is our conversation about those objections, and about the exciting new biology of aging.

Ross Andersen: People usually regard life extension as a futuristic technology, but you begin your paper by discussing the ways that we've already extended the human lifespan. What's driven that?

Bennett Foddy: The reason I present it that way, is that there's always this background moral objection in enhancement debates, where a technology is perceived to be new, and by virtue of being new, is depicted as threatening or even strange. That goes for everything from genetic engineering to steroids to cloning and on and on. I think it's always worth contextualizing these things in terms of the normal. So with human cloning it's worth remembering that it's exactly the same as twinning. With steroids, it's worth remembering that in many ways it's not that different from training and exercise, and also that people have been taking testosterone since ancient times. I think this way you can kind of resist the idea that something is wrong just because it's strange.

When you're talking about medicines that help us live longer, it's important to realize how much we've already accomplished. In the last 150 years or so, we've doubled our life span from 40 to 80 years, and that's primarily through the use of things you can characterize as being medical science. In some cases it's clear that we're talking about medical enhancement—vaccines, for instance, or surgical hygiene and sterilization. And then more broadly there are other, non-medical things like the sanitation of the water supply and the pasteurization of milk and cheese. All of these things have saved an enormous amount of life.

Aging can evolve differently in different species.

The Changing Demographics of Death

It used to be that people would die of an infectious disease; they'd be struck down when they were very young or when they were older and their immune system was weak. Now almost nobody in the first world dies of infectious disease; we've basically managed to completely eradicate infectious disease through medical science. If, at the outset of this process, you asked people if we should develop technologies that would make us live until we're 80 on average instead of until we're 40, people might have expressed these same kind of misgivings that you hear today. They might have said, "Oh no that would be way too long, that would be unnatural, let's not do that."

So, in a way, we shouldn't view it as being extremely strange to develop these medicines, but in another sense we're at a new stage now, because now we're at the forefront of having medicines that actually address the aging process. And that's what I'm interested in talking about—the kinds of medicines that actually slow down the aging process, or at least some of the mechanisms of aging.

Can you explain how senescence, the biological process of aging, is unevenly distributed across species?

There are different animals that are affected differently by various processes of aging. In my paper I go into the case of the American Lobster, which lives about as long as a human being. When you dissect one of these lobsters at the end of its life, its body doesn't show much in the way of weakening or wasting like you see in a human body of advanced age. That suggests that aging can evolve differently in different species. Lobsters seem to have evolved an adaptation against the cellular lifespan. There's this phenomenon where the DNA in our cells basically unravel after they've divided a certain amount of times, but lobsters have this enzyme that helps them replenish their telomeres—the caps that hold DNA together. That's one of the reasons why lobsters don't seem to undergo aging in the same way that we do. . . .

What are the current biological limits on our human life span, or our human "youth span," as you call it—the time that we're able to live as young, vibrant, reproducing individuals?

The sky is sort of the limit there. There won't be a magic pill that gives us infinite youth, but over time there will probably be different technologies that allow you a few extra years of youth. We think of aging as being a unitary thing, but it's made up of hundreds of different processes. So, one of the different things we think about, for example, is dementia, the state where your brain sort of wastes away. Now, if we discover a way of reversing that process, or slowing that process, that would be one dimension where we no longer age, where our minds will stay youthful for longer. It's also possible that we might be able to find a way of stopping people's muscles from wasting away as they get older.

The View from the Future

Nothing is going to be super dramatic, but there will be a point where you'll look back a hundred years and notice that people used to get really kind of feeble and after awhile they weren't capable of really thinking or processing information anymore, and they had to go into a home and they had to be looked after and nursed for a time. And that will seem very old-fashioned and very barbaric, but I very much doubt it will happen at a moment in time where we suddenly realize that some magic pill has exponentially extended our youth. Part of that's because we're not exactly clear what aging is. We've identified a whole range of processes, but there are still a whole lot of arguments in the scientific community about what is really responsible for aging, and which of the processes are subsidiary to other processes.

It makes sense to pursue a youth-extending medicine that would diminish the number of years that we have to spend in nursing homes.

Have we glimpsed, even theoretically, ways that we might add to that youth-span. What are the bleeding edge technologies that might allow us to overcome aging?

I'm not a scientist, so I don't want to weigh in too heavily on somebody's body of research. We've seen promising results looking at the lobsters and we've seen promising results with antioxidants, even aspirin, but as I said these things are going to be incremental. You meet a lot of people in the scientific community that are true believers and they're expecting a kind of a radical thing. And it's not as though we never have a radical thing in medicine, but what we have more frequently is incremental advances. . . .

Some of the biggest strains on our resources stem from the fact that populations are getting older as birthrates go down, especially in the first world. Aging societies are spending more and more on nursing, and so I think that it makes sense to pursue a youth-extending medicine that would diminish the number of years that we have to spend in nursing homes. You could imagine us living more like the lobster, where we still live to be about 80–85, but we're alert and active until we drop dead. In that scenario we wouldn't have this giant burden where the state has to support and pay to nurse people that are unable to look after themselves anymore.

Extending the Lifespan Instead of the Healthspan

Now, it has to be said that the story of medicine and medical progress in the past 50 years has not been heading that way. If anything, we're extending the number of years that we spend needing nursing. We've gotten good at keeping people alive once they're fairly decrepit. And that sort of guarantees that you have the maximum drain on resources, while also producing the kind of minimum amount of human benefit. You get to be 90 years old and your hip goes out, and we give you a massively expensive hip replacement, but we don't do things to prevent your body from wasting away and becoming corroded when you're 20, 30 or 40.

It would be great if everybody could live to be 150, because that would benefit every single person.

There's this great Greek myth, the myth of Tithonus, that always comes to mind. Tithonus was a mortal who was in love with Eos, the goddess of the dawn. Eos didn't want Tithonus to grow old and die, so she went to Zeus to ask for eternal life, which was granted. But, she forgot to ask for eternal youth, and so Tithonus just gets older and older and more decrepit, and eventually he can't really move, and then finally he turns into a grasshopper in the end. That's sort of the course that we're on with our current approach to medicine and life extension.

Distributive Justice

Some ethicists have pointed out that death is one of the major forces for equality in the world, and that welfare disparities will be worsened if some people can afford to postpone old age, or avoid it altogether, while others are unable to. What do you say to them?

I think that's right. I mean there are concerns whenever we develop any kind of medicine or any kind of technology— the concern that these things are going to widen welfare gaps. The story of industrialization is that the people who could afford the cars and machines and factories in Western countries were able to produce a lot more and generate a lot more wealth than people in poorer agrarian economies. That's a serious issue. It's probably true that if people in the first world were, through some sort of medical intervention, able to live to be 200 years old and people in Bangladesh were still dying at a relatively young age, that would tend to widen the distance in personal wealth.

And look this has already happened. It's already unfair that I will on average live to be 80 and yet, if I were born before some arbitrary date, or in some other place, I would live much less longer. Those things are unfair and it's worth worrying about them, but I don't think the correct response is to hold off on the science. It's better if everybody can eventually get this medicine, because living a long time is not a positional good, it's an absolute good. It would be great if everybody could live to be 150, because that would benefit every single person. It's not a good that benefits you only if other people are worse off. When you have goods like that you should try to develop them and then you should worry separately about making sure that they get delivered to people in poorer areas, whether it's through government aid or massive production.

What Role Does Death Play?

Another objection to the elimination of aging is this idea that the aging process makes an elderly person's death less painful for the survivors around her, because it gradually forces people to stop relying on her, and forces her to gradually remove herself from society. You call this the argument from psycho-social history.

This is Leon Kass' argument. He thinks aging is just fantastic for this reason because it helps us to let go of somebody. And of course it's true that when people grow old, they become less useful to society, and more socially difficult, which places burdens on people. And in a lot of cases we respond to this by cutting them out of our lives, essentially. People get older, they move into a nursing home, and we see them less and less, and then when they finally die everyone's like, "well it was expected." Advanced age sort of helps us prepare emotionally for letting go of people, but it seems to me that it's not good for the person who gets old.

I don't think it's ever going to be the case that we live forever.

Now, what would the world be like if people dropped dead in good health when they reach a certain age? It would be very sad, but on the upside the person would've had 20 or 30 years of additional integration into society and we would've been able to spend more time with them. I've got to say that I would've enjoyed my grandmother's presence a lot more if she'd been able to run around and to play and work and be part of society in her extremely advanced age.

The Ultimate Inevitability

Nick Bostrom has said that people have fallen victim to a kind of Stockholm syndrome when it comes to aging. The idea being that because aging has always been an insurmountable obstacle for humanity, that we have dignified it more than it deserves, that we contort ourselves logically and rhetorically to defend it precisely because it is so inescapable. Does that sound right to you?

Yes, I think that's right, although Nick draws conclusions that are a bit more extreme than I would tend to draw. I think that we do have a tendency to kind of rationalize things that we don't think we can do anything about. This is a perfectly healthy attitude if you really can't do anything about the aging process—it's better to accept it and kind of talk about it as being a natural part of life, not something to rail against or feel bad about. It's something that everybody goes through. Now if it did so happen that we could discover a medicine that completely prevents that process from taking place, we would have to re-evaluate at that stage and realize that we've done some emotional rationalization here and the conditions for it no longer apply. We no longer need to comfort ourselves with the inevitability of death if it's not actually inevitable.

Having said that, death is, in fact, inevitable. Even if we solve every medical problem, you still have a 1 in 1,000 chance of dying every year by some sort of accident. So, on those odds you could probably expect to live to be about 1,000. I don't think it's ever going to be the case that we will live forever. It's not even going to be 1,000. We're probably talking about living to be 120 or 150 or somewhere around there, but to me the idea that we have to accept living to 80 rather than 120 is bizarre given that it's not so long ago that we lived to 40.

4

Fears About Radical Life Extension Consequences Are Unrealistic

Sonia Arrison

Sonia Arrison is the author of the book 100+: How the Coming Age of Longevity Will Change Everything, from Careers and Relationships to Family & Faith.

The recent science fiction movie In Time *perpetuates several myths about the consequences of real-life radical life extension. While the movie portrays a dystopian society, in reality extreme longevity is nothing to fear. The movie's scenario of harsh population control is based on mistaken Malthusian beliefs, and real studies show that cutting death rates doesn't increase population very much at all. Likewise, the movie's portrayal of social disruption and income and class disparities misses the mark. In reality, life-extending technologies would become available to everyone in due course because the rich would have a powerful incentive to share them—profit. And rather than the longevity of some coming at the expense of others, in real life everyone would benefit from the increased productivity and creativity. Radical life extension will change the world, but not in the negative way that* In Time *portrays.*

Would the world be a better place if science could stop people from aging? *In Time*, the new sci-fi thriller starring Justin Timberlake and Amanda Seyfried, is based on the

Sonia Arrison, "Don't Be Afraid To Live Longer, Justin Timberlake: What the Dystopian *In Time* Gets Wrong About a World of Extreme Life Extension," *Slate*, October 28, 2011.

outdated idea that longer lives would mean chaos. The film imagines a world in which somatic aging has been engineered to stop at 25; after that, a person is given just one year's worth of time and must earn more by working, and the minutes tick by on a display embedded in his arm. Once someone's clock runs out, he or she literally "times out" and dies. What's more, time serves as money—the longer you have on your life clock, the richer you are.

While the film's fun, it falls into a dystopian trap, assuming that greater longevity would create a terrifying society. But it gets almost everything about human life extension wrong. Scientists are on the verge of discovering ways to radically extend human life—though they probably won't figure out how to maintain the pristine looks of 25-year-olds any time soon. *In Time* seems to argue that we should be concerned about this looming longevity. But there's nothing to be afraid of.

Heavy population growth actually comes from births, not from fewer deaths.

Timberlake's character, Will Salas, is a working-class man who lives in the ghetto and barely scrapes by, earning just enough time to make it to work the next day—bringing new meaning to "living paycheck to paycheck." One night, he meets a wealthy centenarian suffering from an acute case of rich guilt. He opens Salas' eyes to the depths of the time system's inequities: The rich can live forever because they oppress the poor. "Everyone can't live forever," Hamilton explains. "Where would we put them?. . . How else can there be men with a million years when most live day to day?" After Hamilton commits suicide and gifts his vast amounts of remaining time to Salas, Timberlake becomes a fugitive as police assume foul play.

The Population Growth Question

In Time's perhaps most frightening assertion is that an age of extended longevity would require strict population controls (i.e., death) to combat overcrowding and resource depletion. (Indeed, even this week [October 2011] we are seeing renewed concern about overpopulation, as the global head count hits 7 billion.) But this is premised on mistaken Malthusian beliefs that humans consume more than they produce. Sure, if people don't die at the same rate as they do today, then the population may go up (depending on fertility rates), but by how much? The answer might surprise you.

Scholars at the University of Chicago have approached the population/longevity question in an interesting way. If the entire population of Sweden were to become immortal, they asked, how much would population increase? Their model suggests that Sweden's population would increase by only 22 per-cent over 100 years. (For comparison's sake, the number of people in Sweden grew from 5.1 million in 1900 to 8.8 million in 2000, or 57 percent.) One of the reasons that cutting death rates doesn't affect population as much as we might think is that heavy population growth actually comes from births, not from fewer deaths.

Rich vs. Poor?

So let's say the earth can handle people living longer. What about the movie's claim that the wealthy will have access to longer life, but the poor will not? The sad fact is that that is already the case, to a less dramatic extent: A Native American man living in South Dakota has a life expectancy of about 58 years, while an Asian-American woman in New Jersey has a life expectancy of 91 years.

As breakthrough longevity technologies become available, the rich will certainly be the first to partake; they are the ones who will pay most of the early fixed costs for everything from flat-screen TVs to experimental medical treatments. Eventually, these life-extenders will reach everyone. The question is, how long will it take? If the gap between the fountain of longevity's availability for the wealthy and accessibility for the poor is a negligible amount of time, the transition to a long-lived population will be smooth. But if the trickle-down takes a long time, we may indeed face serious social disruption— but not exactly the way *In Time* suggests. The movie assumes that large groups of people who know their lives could be saved will be complacent about their unnecessary deaths. In reality, those people could pick up arms and literally fight for their lives. Luckily, that scenario seems unlikely, thanks to technological progress.

Historically, the time necessary to distribute new technologies across socioeconomic borders has been speeding up. For instance, it took 46 years for one-quarter of the U.S. population to get electricity and 35 years for the telephone to get that far. But it took only 16 years for one-quarter of American households to get a personal computer, 13 years for a cellphone, and seven years for Internet access, a promising trend for those who wish to see the widespread use of longevity technologies. Yes, these examples are all communication innovations—but actually, health technologies themselves are fast becoming information technologies. Just like computers have a code based on 1s and 0s, so too do humans have a code, based on DNA. For example, prices for human genome sequencing are falling, which will make personalized medicines—one potential source of extended lifespans—cheaper in the future. Even if there is a gap between the life expectancy of the rich and the poor, it likely would not be a case of the rich gaining extra years at the expense of the underprivileged. Instead, the opposite is true: The rich have an incentive to make the technologies accessible to everyone, because that means more customers. Hoarding the technology would offer no advantages and would result in an unstable world.

The last major flaw of *In Time*'s long-living world is its portrayal of the economy as a zero-sum game. If one person gets more time, it is at the expense of others. Rather than expanding, the economy just shifts a fixed set of resources from one place to another.

There will be a day in the not-too-distant future when life expectancy . . . is 150 years.

Time Equals Opportunity

In reality, individuals innovate and economies grow, allowing more people to prosper than in the past. But people don't seem to innovate in the film's world, either because they are so distressed about living day-to-day or because they are so rich that they won't try anything new for fear of losing their long lives. (Even those with scads of time left on their clock can die by misadventure, so we see a wealthy girl, played by Amanda Seyfried, who is terrified of going into the ocean and drowning.) As one character puts it, "The poor die and the rich don't live."

The knowledge that time is limited should instead tilt things in favor of enhanced ambition. More time means more opportunity. And, despite well-publicized stories of young tech entrepreneurs creating the next big thing, the reality is that innovation is a late-peak field. Leonardo da Vinci was 51 years old when he started painting the Mona Lisa, and Wilhelm Conrad Röntgen was 50 when he discovered the X-ray. Though they might seem middle-aged by our current standards, they were actually on the elderly side for their time periods. Benjamin Franklin was 46 when he conducted his famous kite experiment verifying the nature of electricity, but he didn't stop there. He was 55 when he invented the glass harmonica and 78 when he invented bifocals. If Franklin had the opportunity to live longer in a healthier state, one wonders what else he would have contributed to society.

During the Cro-Magnon era, human life expectancy was a meager 18 years. By the time of the European Renaissance, one could expect 30 birthdays; by 1850, life expectancy had risen to 43 years. Now, those born in Western societies can expect close to 80 birthdays and look forward to more as science and technology advance.

Fact Not Fiction

These gains are stunning, but even bigger possibilities await. There will be a day in the not-too-distant future when life expectancy—and, more importantly, health expectancy—is 150 years. It won't stop there, of course, but that is what is in our near-term view. That doesn't mean the world will be problem-free or that core tensions between people will disappear. Indeed, in a world where people are around for longer, relationship issues may be more pronounced. (Get ready to deal with a great-grandmother-in-law.) Young workers entering the workforce will have to battle supercentenarians who have no urge to retire. We may face new and troubling types of pollution and perhaps epidemics that we cannot yet fathom.

Being around to witness those problems will be exciting and challenging, but it won't be anything like the scenario portrayed in *In Time.*

5

Radical Life Extension Is Ethical

Russell Blackford

Russell Blackford is a fellow of the Institute for Ethics and Emerging Technologies, a nonprofit that advocates for a responsible, constructive approach to emerging human enhancement technologies. He is a conjoint lecturer in the School of Humanities and Social Science at the University of Newcastle in Australia.

In the early 1990s, bioethicist Peter Singer wrote a paper in which he presented a hypothetical thought experiment: if a new pill could double human life expectancy to 150 years but would lower a person's late-life happiness somewhat, would it be ethical to develop such a pill? After weighing a variety of factors, Singer concluded that it would not be ethical to create such a life-extending treatment under the circumstances he proposed. The following viewpoint is a modern rebuttal to Singer's paper; the author comes to the opposite conclusion by arguing that it is the quality and outcome of individual lives that should matter, not the largest possible sum of population happiness.

Editor's Note: Peter Singer is professor of bioethics at Princeton University and laureate professor at the University of Melbourne.

The current (December 2009) issue of *The Journal of Medical Ethics* contains my paper: "Moral pluralism versus the total view: why Singer is wrong about radical life extension."

There, I critique an early 1990s paper by [bioethicist] Peter Singer, which argues that we should not proceed to develop a hypothetical life-extension drug, based on a scenario where developing the drug would fail to achieve the greatest sum of universal happiness over time. I respond that this is the wrong test. If we ask, more simply, which policy would be more benevolent, we reach a different conclusion from Singer's: even given his questionable scenario, development of the drug should go ahead. A more pluralistic account of the nature of morality than used by Singer reaches a benevolent recommendation on life-extension technology.

My paper is intended not merely to offer a better solution to the conundrums raised in Singer's original piece, but also to suggest a methodology of much wider value in applied moral philosophy.

The Scenario

Singer's argument employs an imaginary scenario in which life extension would not increase, and would actually reduce, the universal sum of happiness or welfare (henceforth, I will refer simply to "happiness") over time. Singer describes a scenario in which an anti-ageing, or life-extension, pill would more-or-less double human lifespans, but the level of happiness enjoyed in the second half of a typical individual's life would be lowered to some (relatively small) extent. He also stipulates that it would be necessary to ensure that fewer people came into existence over time if the life-extending pill were developed and used. Given this scenario, he thinks, we should not go ahead with developmental work on the hypothetical life-extension pill.

More specifically, Singer imagines a scenario in which those who take the drug experience no effect during their early decades of life. However, when they reach middle age, the drug retards further ageing so dramatically as to extend an average life span from about 75 years to about 150 years. During her additional years of life, an individual's health will not be restored to youthful levels, but it will be good enough for a very worthwhile quality of life (similar to the health of people in their sixties or seventies today). An individual may find that life has lost some of its experienced "freshness", and the combination of this (should it happen) with somewhat reduced health will make her additional years less happy than her first 70 or 80 years of life—but not greatly so.

It is easy to demonstrate that, if we adopt all [of Singer's] assumptions . . . the total sum of happiness, over a set period of time, is greater in a society without the life-extension pill than a society with the life extension pill.

[Bioethicist] Mark Walker has questioned this scenario elsewhere, suggesting that it is unrealistic to assume that the first 70 or 80 years would typically be happier than the second for those with what he calls "superlongevity". My own approach is more fundamental, as I conclude that Singer gives the wrong recommendation *even if we accept all of his stipulated facts.*

Additional Assumptions

A further stipulation made by Singer is that resource limitations will require population controls, whether or not the drug becomes generally available, but they will need to be more severe if the pill is developed. Fortunately, Singer tells us, the pill will allow for an increase in average child-bearing age and a lower fertility rate. Nothing in his analysis depends on the exact ingredients of a population policy; rather, his essential point is that it will be necessary to devise an appropriate policy to ensure that only half as many people are born if the life-extension drug is available. I.e., he has in mind a scenario in which the total number of people who will be born and live out their lives over a large number of years will be half what it would have been without the drug. . . .

It is easy to demonstrate that, if we adopt all these assumptions—which Singer evidently regards as constituting a plausible scenario—the total sum of happiness, over a set period of time, is greater in a society *without* the life-extension pill than a society *with* the life extension pill. Moreover, the average society-wide happiness *at any given moment* is higher in the society without the life-extension pill. On the other hand, typical individuals of the future will have better lives in the society with the life-extension pill than in the society without it. This may seem paradoxical, but it is actually quite easy to demonstrate that it is true so long as we make some plausible assumptions. In that case, should we go ahead with developing the drug or not?

We should not try to maximise the overall number of happiness-years. We should try to produce the most fortunate lives.

Differing Views

Singer argues that [we] should not develop the drug; I disagree. But here the argument gets complex, and I cannot, in a relatively brief blog post, do justice to the complex issues that I needed a 7000-word article to tease out properly. I agree with Singer that we should take into account the interests of future generations, not just the interests of people who are alive now, but what follows from this?

It appears that Singer wants to maximise what we could call total future happiness-years (I hope the meaning of this is transparent: in any event, it involves multiplying the number of future people by the average number of years they live, and then by their average level of happiness across an entire life). He wants to do this at all costs, even if the people who come into existence have worse lives than the smaller number of longer-lived of people who would have come into existence under a different policy. I find that very implausible. Although Singer offers thought experiments to support his approach to the question, I find them unconvincing. . . .

We should, I suggest, adopt the more *benevolent* policy, and we should not think of benevolence as a matter of maximising total happiness-years. In a situation such as the one that concerns us, the choice of the pro-pill and anti-pill versions of Singer's life-extension scenario, we should not try to maximise the overall number of happiness-years. We should try to produce the most fortunate lives.

Moral Theories

It may be that utilitarians, such as Peter Singer, are inevitably pushed toward "total-view" thinking—which attempts to maximise the total amount of happiness in the universe—rather than toward a view that we should ensure the best possible lives for those people who will come to exist in the future. As a result utilitarians can, again paradoxically given the sympathies that underly their moral theory, make policy recommendations that are not the most benevolent available.

Unfortunately, all utilitarian theories developed to date contain paradoxes or involve counterintuitive implications. If, however, we take a more pluralistic approach to the sources of our morality, such difficulties vanish. I expect that a considerable diversity of values underpins our actual moral thinking. We care, for example, about the reduction of suffering, about the lives of others going well, and about people being able to live with a certain spontaneity. We value wilderness, art and culture, the quest for knowledge, the existence of complex, creative cultures . . . and many other things. To at least some extent, we value all these for themselves, not solely because of their further utilitarian effects.

We do *not* value the largest possible sum of happiness over time . . . which can, in principle, be gained by multiplying *the number* of sentient beings (so long as they have lives that are at least worth living). What we value, rather, is that *whatever actual lives come into being should go well.* Other things being equal, we value the outcomes that would be chosen, among those possible, by a benevolent decision-maker, not by a decision-maker committed to total-view utilitarianism. As shown by the way Singer has set up his life-extension scenario, these two kinds of outcomes can diverge.

The Life Extension Pill Should Proceed

It is clear to me that I should vote to go ahead and develop the life-extension pill—and so, after reflection, should you, and so should Singer. No plausible values are violated by this action; quite the opposite. Far from feeling guilt or regret at having adversely affected another person, or having destroyed or damaged anything precious, an individual who votes to develop the life-extension pill has every reason to feel virtuous. She will have helped to create a world in which lives go better than (more and different) lives would otherwise have.

6

Life Extension Medicine Can Be Dangerous

Arlene Weintraub, interviewed by Christie Findlay

Arlene Weintraub is a writer specializing in pharmaceuticals, health care, and biotechnology. Her book about the anti-aging industry, Selling the Fountain of Youth, *was published in 2010. Christie Findlay is a staff writer for the* AARP Bulletin, *a monthly publication by AARP, the nation's largest membership organization and advocacy group for senior citizens.*

Anti-aging medicine has grown into a booming $88 billion industry, but the public is being misled about both the safety and the effectiveness of the treatments. Many anti-aging products are based on steroids, human growth hormone, and bioidentical hormones—hormones from plants and other sources that are purportedly identical to what the body produces. Anti-aging doctors say these substances can help the body repair itself and become more youthful, and that because they are "natural," they are safe to use indefinitely. Mainstream doctors, however, believe that many of the substances are dangerous and that the public is being misled because the risks of using such products are not properly explained. Celebrity endorsements of anti-aging regimens deepen the problem by giving unproven and unsafe therapies added credibility and publicity.

Would you like to be able to jump out of bed, play tennis with your grandchildren, or have the best sex of your life? Antiaging doctors say they've finally found the secret.

Christie Findlay, "The Author Speaks: The Dangers of Trying to Live Forever: Interview with *Selling the Fountain of Youth* Author, Arlene Weintraub," *AARP Bulletin*, January 13, 2011. Copyright © 2011 by AARP. All rights reserved. Reproduced by permission.

Their go-to treatments are steroids, human growth hormone and bioidentical hormones, which they believe offer a natural way to regain youth. Many aging Americans believe it too, which is why the antiaging business has boomed into an $88 billion industry.

But mainstream scientific researchers say these treatments are unproven and may raise the risk of cancer and other diseases. And watchdog groups accuse antiaging doctors of promoting dangerous treatments without warning patients of potential risks.

Arlene Weintraub, who spent 10 years as a science reporter at *Business Week*, first wrote about antiaging in 2006. Her new book, *Selling the Fountain of Youth: How the Anti-Aging Industry Made a Disease Out of Getting Old—And Made Billions*, takes readers behind the scenes at the aging clinics, compounding pharmacies and for-profit businesses that are working to legitimize antiaging medicine. Prepare to be scared—and challenged—by what she discovered.

A small group of doctors latched on to the idea that if you replace your hormone levels to where they were in your 30s, you'll feel as great as you did back then.

Christie Findlay: What started the modern antiaging movement?

Arlene Weintraub: In 1990, scientist Daniel Rudman published a sensational study. He gave human growth hormone (HGH) to about a dozen healthy men over 60. They significantly increased their lean body mass, including muscle, and they lost about 14 percent of their fat.

How did we get from a single splashy study to an entirely new industry?

A small group of doctors latched on to the idea that if you replace your hormone levels to where they were in your 30s, you'll feel as great as you did back then. Rudman's study inspired the formation of the American Academy of Anti-Aging Medicine and has been cited on the Web something like 50,000 times.

The Anti-Aging Industry

What are the cornerstones of the antiaging industry?

It started with HGH and expanded into alternative estrogen and progesterone products for menopause, as well as testosterone, which has recently become quite a sensation in this industry. It's being prescribed not just to men, but also to help improve women's libido.

What are proponents claiming about these products?

They say if you replace those hormones, you can prevent osteoporosis, shield yourself from Alzheimer's, improve your sleep, lose weight, gain muscle mass and boost your sex drive.

Does any good science support those claims?

Antiaging doctors often say HGH is one of the most studied hormones. Well, that's true, but many of those studies were in children with growth hormone deficiencies, and you can't extrapolate from those children to healthy adults. The original Rudman study of HGH in adults was very small, and some scientists have been disturbed by the popularity of it. Some antiaging doctors twist the research to fit their viewpoints.

Why aren't there any better, more long-term studies?

They're expensive. Also, it's hard to recruit patients without knowing the risks and benefits. And you can't expose patients to something that might be a cancer-causing agent. For example, one study looked at a patient who took HGH for longevity and ended up developing cancer. You can't make a direct link, but there's enough suspicion that it would be unethical to do a longevity study.

Safety Is in Question

What are mainstream doctors' biggest concerns about the safety of antiaging medicine?

One of the biggest safety issues is with the bioidentical hormones, which are supposed to be chemically identical to those your body produces. They're estrogen and progesterone products derived from yams and soybeans. Many neighborhood pharmacists are able to compound their own creams, gels and injectable pellets.

The pharmaceutical industry also offers hormones derived from plant sources, but many antiaging doctors say those versions are synthetic while compounded versions are not. Antiaging doctors say things like, "We've invented these great bioidentical products, they're from nature, they're perfectly safe for you to take the rest of your life."

However, mainstream doctors believe all estrogen is dangerous, regardless of its source, and has the same risks as the standard menopause hormones like Premarin and Prempro, which the Women's Health Initiative showed to raise the risk of breast cancer and stroke.

One of the biggest safety issues is with the bioidentical hormones, which are supposed to be chemically identical to those your body produces.

Why are patients so eagerly embracing unproven treatments that could actually harm them?

They're very popular among the baby boomer generation. They want to keep working or have an active retirement, and don't want to get frail. So they're very eager to try substances even if they might be risky.

It's hard to argue that someone wouldn't want more sex or sleep.

Exactly!

Would you consider wrinkle creams and Botox as risky as bioidentical hormones?

Botox is one of the only FDA [US Food and Drug Administration]-approved antiaging products. Its label contains a lot of warnings, so patients know what they're getting into. The compounded hormones being prescribed for antiaging generally don't offer as much cautionary information.

Why don't they have to carry warning labels?

There's a web of regulations and rulings in this country, including the Dietary Supplement Health and Education Act of 1994, that dictate what compounding pharmacists can and cannot do. But the bottom line is that compounding pharmacists have a lot of freedom. For example, they don't have to include warning labels on their products. That's tragic. They should have to include the same warning labels as pharmaceutical companies when they're using the same chemicals.

Selling Confusion

So drug companies and compounding pharmacies are offering essentially the same products?

Exactly. They're all hormones, just derived from different sources. So women are really confused. They don't know they can get bioidentical hormones that are approved by the FDA and maybe paid for by insurance, because the antiaging industry does such a good job telling them only their compounding pharmacy can make these products.

Antiaging doctors will often tell people it's safe to be on these regimens indefinitely.

Are there any real differences?

Well, the other controversy is that the antiaging industry says you have to have a form of estrogen called estriol, because that's what your body makes naturally. Estriol is not actually in any FDA-approved drugs, so technically, under FDA guidelines, compounding pharmacies are not supposed to be using it in any products. There are some studies showing it to be dangerous. The FDA told me they've had adverse reports of people taking estriol.

If both mainstream medicine and antiaging practitioners are offering virtually the same products, why is there more concern about the antiaging industry's programs?

Antiaging doctors will often tell people it's safe to be on these regimens indefinitely. But the mainstream medical world believes the safest route is to take the smallest dose possible for the shortest amount of time possible. Also, many critics believe antiaging products should carry labels saying things like, "This product contains estrogen and progesterone, which have been tied to breast cancer," or "This product also contains estriol, which is not contained in any FDA-approved product."

Why aren't antiaging doctors telling their patients there are FDA-approved alternatives?

I did meet some ethical doctors who give their patients a choice. But they say, "You can get such-and-such product made by a pharmaceutical company, or you can go to our compounding pharmacy and get something that's tailored just for you."

What Are the Alternatives?

If people are having age-related problems such as muscle loss, energy, hot flashes, libido, sleep, what are some safe alternatives?

Exercise is actually the only thing that's been proven to fend off the aging process. The MacArthur Foundation Study included results of several long-term studies in its book *Successful Aging*. A study out of Texas found that adults who became fit decreased their chances of dying from any disease by 40 percent. And fit doesn't mean Arnold Schwarzenegger; it means walking half an hour three or four times a week.

If people are looking for well-researched medical advice about antiaging medicine, where should they go?

Great resources include the North American Menopause Society, the Endocrine Society, the International Longevity Center, the National Women's Health Network, Public Citizen, and the MacArthur Foundation Research Network on an Aging Society. And the FDA has several helpful pages.

If someone does go see an antiaging doctor, what questions should they ask?

They should ask for studies showing (a) that the treatment will reduce their symptoms or help them live longer, and (b) that they are safe. And get a second opinion from someone who's not an antiaging doctor—maybe an ob-gyn who specializes in serving the aging population.

Some of the women I talked to didn't seem to understand they were taking estrogen. They thought they were taking something that isn't a drug.

It sounds like the Starbucks cure for aging. Why would you get plain old drip coffee when you can order a nonfat, low-sugar vanilla, extra-foam, extra-hot latte.

Plus, I talked to ob-gyns who say you can't tailor products that way. Your hormone levels vary throughout the day, so a single blood or saliva test doesn't tell you much. What they're promising may not be exactly accurate.

Do antiaging patients understand what they're taking?

Some of the women I talked to didn't seem to understand they were taking estrogen. They thought they were taking something that isn't a drug, and it didn't occur to them these products might have any risks.

What surprised you the most while you were reporting this story?

I was shocked by how many doctors are taking these substances themselves. For their patients, it's like, "If my doctor is taking these hormones, how can they be dangerous?"

What types of medicine were most antiaging doctors practicing before specializing in antiaging?

You'll find doctors from all different specialties—from internists to emergency room doctors—but you won't find many endocrinologists in antiaging. Which is ironic, because antiaging focuses on hormone treatment.

Suzanne Somers's Role

Suzanne Somers says her antiaging program is the best thing she's ever done in her life. And she looks as young, beautiful and healthy as she did in her 20s!

She does estrogen, testosterone and HGH, and on *Oprah* last year she showed a line of 60 supplement pills. She's created this perception that compounded bioidentical compounds are not synthetic drugs. I truly think she believes that. But no mainstream doctor would tell patients that hormones are not drugs. So she's created a lot of confusion.

What did you think of that Oprah show?

It was the biggest boost the antiaging industry has ever gotten. Suzanne Somers was on the stage, while the actual medical doctors were sidelined in the audience. I interviewed one of those doctors, Lauren Streicher. She keeps running into situations where Suzanne Somers is shown as the expert, and she—the Northwestern ob-gyn [who teaches at the Feinburg School of Medicine]—is shown as some crazy lady trying to discredit Suzanne Somers!

What do you say to critics who claim you've been compensated by pharmaceutical companies?

I laugh. I'm not sure where they're getting that idea. Some say *Business Week* took pharmaceutical advertising, and therefore I was getting paid by drug companies. But we had a Chinese wall between advertising and editorial, so reporters were never affected by ad sales. What's especially funny is that during my 10 years at *Business Week* I could count our pharmaceutical ads on one hand.

Others say you must have cozy industry ties after covering the health beat for so long.

I actually have a record of not being very kind to the pharmaceutical industry—you can read those stories on my website. I did a series of stories on conflicts of interest in the pharmaceutical industry. And my book takes a harsh look at pharmaceutical companies' marketing of human growth hormone. I also criticize Wyeth for not being entirely honest about selling estriol overseas while fighting its distribution in the U.S.; it looked like Wyeth was just trying to protect its Premarin franchise.

This antiaging obsession makes growing old seem like something to be avoided at all cost. But it's just another part of the human experience.

And there's a school of thought among some doctors that the decline of hormones is protective. Because we see hormones linked to cancer, maybe it's by design that we lose hormones as we age. I personally see aging as a privilege, not something to be avoided.

7

Viable Life Extension Science Fights for Credibility

Ronald Bailey

Ronald Bailey is the science correspondent for Reason *magazine and the author of* Liberation Biology: The Scientific and Moral Case for the Biotech Revolution.

The promise of radically extending the human lifespan is real, and the field of anti-aging research is quickly growing. Scientists are approaching the problem of aging from many different angles, including research into calorie restrictive diets, stem cell therapy, DNA sequencing, cell regeneration, and even nanotechnology. Experts predict that breakthroughs in the field will increase exponentially and that humanity will soon approach "longevity escape velocity"—a state when an individual's day of death moves further away rather than closer. The concept of living hundreds of years still sounds "creepy" to most people, however, and a tidal wave of fraudulent anti-aging treatments and medicines has undermined public confidence in the possibility of developing viable anti-aging therapies. More research and funding is needed to further the progress of legitimate life extension science.

If you're under age 30, it is likely that you will be able to live as long as you want. That is, barring accidents and wars, you have centuries of healthy life ahead of you. So the participants in the Longevity Summit convened in Manhattan Beach, California, contend. Over the weekend [November 2009]

Maximum Life Foundation president David Kekich gathered a group of scientists, entrepreneurs, and visionaries to meet for three days with the goal of developing a scientific and business strategy to make extreme human life extension a real possibility within a couple of decades. Kekich dubbed the effort the "Manhattan Beach Project."

Tech entrepreneur and futurist Ray Kurzweil opened the conference with a virtual presentation on exponential technology trends that are bringing the prospect of achieving longevity escape velocity ever closer. "We are very close to the tipping point in human longevity," asserted Kurzweil to the conferees. "We are about 15 years away from adding more than one year of longevity per year to remaining life expectancy." This has been labeled by summiteer and life-extension guru Aubrey de Grey as *longevity escape velocity*. Achieving escape velocity, according to Kekich, would mean that "your projected day of reckoning moves further away from you rather than closing in on you."

"Health and medicine will be a million times more powerful in 20 years," Kurzweil declared. He predicted that the complexity of biology will yield to the exponential powers of applied information technology and take off. He cited Moore's Law which predicts doubling of microchip functionality and halving their costs every two years.

It is well established that restricting many mammal species to about two-thirds of what they would ordinarily eat extends their healthy lifespans.

Costs Are Declining

The decrease in cost and increase in speed of sequencing whole human genomes is outpacing even Moore's Law. In 2000, the first genome was sequenced after 14 years and at a cost of $3 billion. Now various startups offer the potential to sequence an individual's DNA for less than $100 in under an hour.

The goal of the summit was to devise scientific and business strategies with the goal of demonstrating the capability to reverse aging in an older human being by 2029. By then, Kurzweil argued, people will be beginning their intimate merger with information technologies, biotechnologies, and nanotechnologies. Kurzweil, age 61, emphasized, "Something I am personally interested in is not just designer babies, but designer baby boomers."

Going Back to Move Forward

Anti-aging research is a rich and varied territory right now. Researchers are finally beginning to get a handle on the actual causes of aging. With this increased scientific understanding, some researchers now believe they are on the way to figuring out how to stop it, and—eventually—how to reverse it.

University of California, Riverside biochemist Stephen Spindler reported on his research seeking caloric restriction mimetics. It is well established that restricting many mammal species to about two-thirds of what they would ordinarily eat extends their healthy lifespans. For example, calorie restricted mice live up to 50 percent longer, and experience less heart disease and cancer than those who eat as much as they want. Spindler is now screening a variety of compounds including pharmaceuticals to see if they mimic the effects of calorie restriction in mice. He presented early results that show that some compounds, like cholesterol lowering statin drugs and the immune suppressant rapamycin, do seem to increase mouse lifespans. However, Spindler added that more is not necessarily better. Mice receiving combinations of compounds are not living any longer. "I personally would caution people taking large amounts of supplements in combination to be careful," said Spindler. The good news is that several major pharmaceutical companies are working on calorie restriction mimetics known as sirtuins.

Aging and Natural Selection

Michael Rose, a biologist at the University of California, Irvine, has been breeding long-lived fruit flies to one another for decades. Rose's work is built on the premise that natural selection is the cause of aging. Specifically, natural selection works to keep organisms healthy and alive until after they have reproduced. Once they've reproduced, natural selection no longer works to prevent the accumulation of damage that leads to aging and death. Your body is no longer needed by your germ cells once their genes have moved on to the bodies of your children.

The only cells in our bodies that do not suffer telomere shortening are reproductive cells because the enzyme telomerase keeps adding new repeats as they divide.

Using artificial selection for longevity, Rose has produced fruit flies that live four times longer than normal, the human equivalent of being healthy at age 300. The Methuselah flies are more fecund and better at handling environmental stresses than are normal flies. Since fruit flies and humans share many similar genes, insights garnered from the genomics of long-lived flies are being used by Genescient LLC to develop anti-aging supplements for people. The company plans to release its first product in 2010. "In my world biological immortality is possible," said Rose.

William Andrews, head of Sierra Sciences (motto "Cure Aging or Die Trying") talked about his company's project to identify compounds that lengthen telomeres. Why do that? Telomeres are repeated sequences of DNA that cap the ends of chromosomes to keep them from unraveling and to keep them from binding to other chromosomes. At conception, telomeres are about 15,000 repeats long. Each time a cell divides it loses about 100 repeats, growing ever shorter. When the repeats get short enough, cells generally receive a signal that tells them to die. Andrews argues that telomeres control aging in cells and thus control aging in us. A new study this month [November 2009] reports that centenarians have longer telomeres than controls do.

Testing Telomeres

According to Andrews, when an adult's telomeres get down to about 5,000 repeats they die of old age. By looking at telomere length in a blood sample, Andrews claimed, "I can tell how old you are and how long you have before you die of old age." (For the curious, Spectracell offers a commercial telomere length test.) The only cells in our bodies that do not suffer telomere shortening are reproductive cells because the enzyme telomerase keeps adding new repeats as they divide. The goal of Sierra Sciences is to develop compounds that will reactivate telomerase in somatic cells to stop telomere shortening. After screening more than 160,000 compounds, Sierra has come up with 33 that activate telomerase and lengthen telomeres. "This would be the biggest thing to hit the planet, if we can turn these into drugs,' said Andrews. Also represented at the summit was TA Sciences which manufactures a telomerase activator as a supplement called TA 65, which is derived from the astragalus plant. Cost? A mere $8,000 for a six month supply.

Why do some people live to be over 100 years old? That's the question that Stephen Coles, head of the Supercentenarian Research Foundation (SRF) is trying to answer. Supercentenarians are people who are over 110 years old. In the world there are 76 currently validated supercentenarians, 72 are female and 4 are male. The genetic underpinnings of their longer lives are still murky. However, Coles has performed a number of autopsies and he has found that most died of senile cardiac amyloidosis, the accumulation of amyloid fibers in their heart muscles.

Supercentenarians and Stem Cells

John Furber, founder of Legendary Pharmaceuticals, discussed the problem of accumulating crosslinked proteins and sugars inside and outside of cells, e.g., fibers like those that killed Coles' supercentenarians. The digestive organelles inside cells called lysosomes slowly become clogged with advanced glycation end-products (AGEs). The promise of one product that aimed to break up damaging crosslinks, alagebrium, has faded with the financial prospects of the company that developed it. If old fibroblasts, the cells that produce connective fibers, could be rejuvenated, say by restoring their telomere lengths, then, perhaps drug interventions like alagebrium might not be needed. Interestingly, there is some evidence that periodic fasting upregulates autophagy, the process by which cells digest accumulating cellular and extracellular junk.

Anti-aging research is not for the faint-hearted. Biologist Michael West was one of the founders of the biotech stem cell company Geron. He later founded Advanced Cell Technology which worked on therapeutic cloning. Therapeutic cloning, a.k.a somatic cell nuclear transfer, involves inserting nuclei from specific patients into human eggs to produce stem cells that are immunologically matched to those patients. The goal would be to transform these stem cells into other cells—nerve, muscle, immune system cells—which could be used to repair damaged or old tissues and organs.

That's the theory, but no one has been able to perfect the practice; no stem cell lines have been derived from cloned human embryos so far. West now heads up BioTime, which is increasingly focused on using induced pluripotent stem cells (IPS cells).

IPS cells are created by dosing normal adult cells, say skin cells, taken from a patient with various embryonic factors that cause it to revert to an earlier stage of development. IPS cells can be transformed into other types of cells which can be used to repair damage or rejuvenate tissues and organs. For example, new hemangioblasts, the precursor cells of blood, could be used to reconstitute and rejuvenate the human immune system.

Anti-aging research is not for the faint-hearted.

DNA Research and Freezing Organs

Former biotech company founder Robert Bradbury proposed that the accumulation of misrepaired double strand breaks in the DNA that makes up our genes as a significant cause of aging. If a single strand is broken, the second strand functions as a template for guiding the proper repair of the broken one. Misrepaired genes make distorted proteins which do not work as well or not at all. By age 70, each cell averages several thousand double strand breaks. However, some cells are unscathed by these breaks. Bradbury is developing techniques to identify these "pristine stem cells" which he believes may be used to grow new organs and tissues to replace damaged or old ones. He points out that there are some 2,600 stem cell therapy trials currently underway in the U.S.

Gregory Fahy, the chief scientific officer of 21st Century Medicine, is working on the cryopreservation of tissues and organs. Fahy pointed out that about one-third of people die of organ failure, e.g., heart attacks, kidney failure, and the like. The problem is that the ice crystals that form during freezing damage organs a lot. His company has developed a number of low toxicity cryoprotectants which enable the vitrification of organs as they cool. Vitrification prevents the formation of ice crystals and thus limits freeze damage. Vitrified corneal cells transplanted into the eyes of vervet monkeys work. Fahy has successfully transplanted a dog kidney kept at 0 degrees Celsius for four days.

SENS Foundation Efforts

Theoretical biogerontologist, Aubrey de Grey, the founder of the SENS Foundation and the Methuselah Foundation, is the energizer bunny of anti-aging scientific research and advocacy. SENS stands for Strategies for Engineered Negligible Senescence, which de Grey defines as "an integrated set of medical techniques designed to restore youthful molecular and cellular structure to aged tissues and organs." De Grey focused on one proposed anti-aging solution which is to install mitochondrial genes in the nuclei of cells. One theory of aging is that the cellular powerhouses, the mitochondria, produce highly reactive molecules called free radicals as a side effect of generating energy to run cells. These free radicals over time cause mutations in mitochondrial genes which become ever more damaged, producing even more free radicals in a downward death spiral. If these mitochondrial genes could be moved to the more protected nucleus this free radical death spiral could be greatly attenuated. Engineering this migration from mitochondria to nucleus has been successful for one gene so far.

De Grey also addressed the problem of eliminating the damaging crosslinked proteins and sugars that clog cells and damage the extracellular matrix. The SENS Foundation is funding research to find enzymes in bacteria that degrade these organic complexes with the goal of turning them into drugs.

Beyond Biology

One major barrier to cracking the problem of aging is a shortage of researchers. Computer scientist Peter Voss, the founder of Adaptive Artificial Intelligence, aims to solve that researcher shortage by creating the equivalent of thousands of researchers and research assistants by means of artificial general intelligence. "Imagine hundreds of thousands of Ph.D.-level machines chipping away at the aging problem," mused Voss. Two years ago at the Singularity Summit, Voss declared, "In my opinion AIs will be developed almost certainly in less than 10 years and quite likely in less than five years." At the Longevity Summit, Voss predicted that his artificially intelligent researchers would be ready in six years.

Biology is nanotechnology that works. Robert Freitas and Ralph Merkle, from the Institute for Molecular Manufacturing, outlined their vision of how a robust medical non-biological nanotechnology would work in 20 years or so. Freitas won the 2009 Feynman Prize for Theory, in recognition of his pioneering work in molecular mechanosynthesis. Nanotechnology aims to control matter at the atomic and molecular scale. "The difference between good and bad health is how your atoms are arranged," pronounced Merkle.

The goal of medical nanotechnology is to unleash exceedingly tiny machines to patrol throughout the body and its cells repairing damage as it occurs. They envision respirocytes to carry oxygen more efficiently than red blood cells; microbivores to attack and digest pathogens; and even chromallocytes to repair and replace damaged chromosomes.

One major barrier to cracking the problem of aging is a shortage of researchers.

In his presentation Kurzweil envisioned constant nanotech monitoring of individual brain cells. Such nanotech devices would "ultimately capture our mind files and back them up," suggested Kurzweil. "A thousand years from now, people will think it pretty daunting the people today went through life without backing up their mind files every day."

But what if you don't live long enough to take advantage of the new longevity treatments coming along in a couple of decades? For example, this life expectancy calculator suggests that there is a 50 percent chance that I will live only another 33 years. Kekich, who convened the summit, urged participants to take good care of their health—diet, exercise, supplements, stress management—because they are not gambling on just 15 years more of life, but perhaps 1,500 years of life.

Life After Death?

But what if the grim reaper comes despite your best efforts to stave him off?

Ralph Merkle, in his role as a board member of the Alcor Life Extension Foundation, explained the goal of cryonics. Cryonics involves storing human bodies or brains at the temperature of liquid nitrogen (320 degrees below zero Fahrenheit). Alcor defines cryonics as "a speculative life support technology that seeks to preserve human life in a state that will be viable and treatable by future medicine." Or as Merkle put it, "We want a second opinion from a future physician." The idea is that if brain structure is preserved, nanomedical devices would be able to restore a person to life sometime in the future. Merkle acknowledges that cryonics is highly experimental (to say the least), but we do also know what happens to the control group. Merkle ended with his standard quip, "So you have to decide if you want to be in the experimental group or the control group."

Immortality, Inc.

Some [of] the brainstormers in the business strategy session of the Manhattan Beach Project were new media entrepreneur and Disney executive Oliver Luckett, 2008 Libertarian Party VP candidate Wayne Allyn Root, computer and biotech entrepreneur Richard Offerdahl, marketing expert John Lustyan, social media marketer Michael Terpin, Lifestar Institute COO Kevin Perrott, CEO of TA Sciences Noel Patton, filmmaker

Michael Potter, marketer Joe Sugarman, computer entrepreneur Ken Weiss, and Bill Faloon, co-founder of the Life Extension Foundation.

Hanging over the entire event was a single question: Why are so many people unaware of the tantalizing possibility of soon achieving extreme human life extension? And why do so many reject it when they hear about it? Luckett put his finger exactly on the chief problem. Aspiring to live for hundreds of years sounds creepy to most people. And the longevity "space" is filled nearly to the brim with scammers and charlatans, peddling all manner of 21st century snake oils.

To illustrate the creep-out factor, Luckett told the story of offering the trailer to the documentary about Ray Kurzweil, *Transcendent Man*, to run on his father's campaign website (his father [Bill Luckett] is running for governor of Mississippi [in 2011]). The campaign handlers took one look at it and said, "Keep that trailer as far away as possible. We can't have a trailer talking about transcending religion being shown at the local Baptist church."

Will you be part of the last generation to die from aging, or will you be part of the first generation to enjoy open-ended youth and vitality?

As someone who has leveraged social media into several businesses, Luckett urged summiteers to focus their efforts on spreading their message using those new communications technologies. People trust new ideas that come from their friends. Of course, social media "friends" now include stars and athletes. Being in Tinsel Town, the assembled marketers spent some time brainstorming about which film or TV stars might take up the cause of promoting longevity research. Apparently, Suzanne Summers is an enthusiast, but I sure hope that the summiteers can find some other celebrities.

A Call for Funding

The summiteers also puzzled over the frustrating fact that no billionaire evidently wants to live forever. Why else have none come forward to finance serious life extension research? Entrepreneur Offerdahl explained that rich people fear the ridicule of their friends. Longevity quackery is rife and rich folks don't want to suffer embarrassment in front their friends who would accuse them of being dupes. Like all non-profit efforts, the summiteers longed to find one billionaire who would risk ridicule to support serious life extension research.

How much cash is needed to get a good start on the goal of stopping aging by 2024 and demonstrating that it can be reversed by 2029? Kekich crunched numbers to come with a figure of a mere $63 million to jump start a future of perpetual youth. Of course some avenues are already being explored by well-funded biotech and pharmaceutical companies, e.g. calorie restriction mimetics like sirtuins. After batting around a few ideas, the group finally focused on a proposal by Bill Faloon to create a public life extension research company. The goal of the corporation would be to raise money to invest specifically in companies that research technologies aiming to stop and reverse aging, not just treat diseases. The Manhattan Beach Project participants would seek to raise an initial $5 million before bringing the company to the public. Faloon and another participant committed a million dollars to the project. One idea was to call it MaxLife Capital, but my favorite proposed corporate moniker was Immortality, Inc.

At the end of the summit, David Kekich's poignant question still resonates: "Will you be part of the last generation to die from aging, or will you be part the first generation to enjoy open-ended youth and vitality?"

8

Reasons and Methods for Promoting Our Duty to Extend Healthy Life Indefinitely

Aubrey de Grey

Biomedical gerontologist and radical life extension proponent Aubrey D.N.J. de Grey is founder of the SENS Research Foundation, a nonprofit whose mission is to develop, promote, and ensure access to rejuvenation biotechnologies that target the disabilities and diseases of aging. SENS is an acronym for "Strategies for Engineered Negligible Senescence." De Grey is also chairman and chief science officer of the Methuselah Foundation, a nonprofit working to find a cure for age-related disease.

Many people—both bioethicists and members of the general public—have the perception that aging is somehow different from other causes of disease and death; that is why few people recognize a moral duty to fight aging and seek a cure for it as they would for cancer or some other ailment. The reasoning they use to exempt aging from the moral imperative of scientific pursuit is faulty at its core. An approach to logical arguments known as "reflective equilibrium" has the best chance to sway opinion on the matter. It is important to do so because aging must be fought to the best of human ability, and science has a clear moral duty to extend the human lifespan indefinitely.

Aubrey de Grey, "Reasons and Methods for Promoting Our Duty to Extend Healthy Life Indefinitely," *Journal of Evolution and Technology*, vol. 18, no. 1, May 2008, pp. 50–55.

Abstract

A pervasive reaction to the idea of extreme or indefinite postponement of human aging—one heard from many professional bioethicists and also from a high proportion of the general public—is that aging differs morally from other causes of debilitation and death in a manner that exempts us from the duty to combat it that we perceive as so self-evident in respect of those other causes. Precisely what characteristic of aging underpins this alleged distinction? I argue here that it is in fact a false distinction, perpetuated only by unwarranted psychological forces posing as philosophical arguments. In particular, I note that even an argument based ultimately on the currently unpopular meta-ethical concept of non-cognitivism cannot logically permit one to regard aging as a phenomenon that we can morally desist from combating to the best of our ability. I conclude that a cognitivism-agnostic line of reasoning, based on reflective equilibrium, offers the best chance for influencing hearts and minds on this issue in the near term.

The Pro-Aging Flight from Reason

It is hardly necessary in this essay to enumerate the plethora of almost comically irrational defences of aging that are commonly encountered when the topic of extreme life extension arises in casual conversation (de Grey 2003). All that is really worth mentioning here is that the irrationality of most of these reactions primarily resides not in their inherent validity as concerns, but rather in the certainty with which their exponents present them as supposedly obvious proofs that the elimination of aging would make life not worth living. There is no doubt that a post-aging world will be radically different from today's, and indeed that some of the differences merit extensive forward-planning to minimise their drawbacks (particular the drawbacks that may accompany the *transition* to the post-aging state). Thus, if someone who may hitherto have applied only minimal thought to the topic raises concerns as to whether issues such as inequality of access, boredom or cognitive ossification might merit caution, they do not thereby identify themselves as having abandoned the respect for rationality that constitutes the central prerequisite for any productive debate. Rather, such people often turn out to be quite receptive (albeit perhaps not instantly) to the simple and highly compelling arguments, surely familiar to all readers, that demonstrate the moral equivalence of combating aging and combating the panoply of other causes of suffering and death that are rather more rarely defended in modern society. No—the problem is that, all too often, these conversations never attain the level of objectivity necessary for such arguments to be rehearsed at all. Rather, defenders of aging frequently exhibit from the outset a lack of sincere interest in the question: a determination either to change the subject, or to restrict the conversation to an exchange of witticisms, or even to cast their interlocutor as a dangerous dreamer or ignoramus, so fixated by the lure of scientific and technological progress as to have abandoned all sense of ethical propriety.

When earnest debate is resisted, options for how to proceed are usually limited. In this case, however, the situation is in my view not so bleak. The feature that I perceive as providing a constructive and promising way forward is one that is popularly viewed as being just the opposite, an obstacle to progress. This is the presence in the debate of a number of highly articulate and prominent theologians and ethicists who sincerely propound the pro-aging position and claim to be able to defend it against the arguments alluded to above (President' Council 2003).

The Paradoxical Utility of Bioconservatives

One might initially suppose that the ideal spectrum of academic opinion on a topic that divides society is a consensus in favour of the "correct" opinion. When the topic really does divide society, that may be true—but this is not such a case.

The problem for those of us who are not in favour of aging is that, sad to say, there is an overwhelming preponderance of opinion (essentially a consensus) within society that aging is, if not a good thing, then at least something opposition to which must be viewed with grave suspicion. In this situation, I believe that the existence of a wide spectrum of opinion within academia is actually preferable to the alternative in which opposite consensi exist within academia and among the general public, because that latter situation does not encourage anyone in either community to engage in sincere discourse. When academia is split, by contrast, such discourse will occur—and it will be public and publicised, so it will inform and eventually affect public opinion.

The above line of reasoning has become particularly apposite during the tenure of George W. Bush in the White House and the contemporaneous elevation of Leon Kass to a position of influence arguably not enjoyed by any bioethicist for a century. Kass has spent his entire academic career at the forefront of the battle against biomedical progress, starting with in vitro fertilisation in the 1970s (Kass 1971). His installation by Bush as chair of the President's Council on Bioethics surely resulted not only from this, however, but also from his exceptional skill at conveying his point of view in a language that the general public seems to find attractive.

The Rhetorical Wisdom of the Wisdom of Repugnance

In 1997, Leon Kass published in The New Republic an essay entitled "The wisdom of repugnance" in which he presented his reasons for opposing human reproductive cloning (Kass 1997). In a nutshell, his core argument was that the objective reasons why this procedure is morally unacceptable are of secondary importance in the process of determining that it indeed is unacceptable. Rather, what matters most is that human reproductive cloning is "repugnant" and that this gut reaction can safely be relied upon to cast human reproductive cloning as morally unacceptable. In Kass's words, "repugnance is the emotional expression of deep wisdom, beyond reason's power fully to articulate it."

What are we to make of this position? It bears analysis for two sharply contrasting reasons.

The first is its meta-ethical status. A dominant view within ethics nowadays, cognitivism, is that propositions concerning the moral acceptability or imperative of particular actions have objective truth values, independent of the existence of minds that agree or disagree with those propositions. The opposing view, non-cognitivism, is that no such objective morality exists: a certain action may be morally unacceptable to one agent, acceptable to another and morally imperative to a third, without any of them being objectively incorrect. Now: either a cognitivist or a non-cognitivist could, in principle, either agree or disagree with Kass's position that repugnance is reliable, because that position concerns the methods by which we discover what is right and what is wrong, which is formally independent of whether such rightness or wrongness is objective. However, I would suggest that in practice a cognitivist cannot agree with Kass on this point. The idea that an objective truth can reliably be discovered by examining one's emotions is surely far-fetched. Thus, I claim that Kass is implicitly espousing a clear non-cognitivist meta-ethical position here—a position which, as just mentioned, currently enjoys little support within his field.

The second reason for examining Kass's reliance on repugnance is its rhetorical status. This particular essay remains among Kass's most high-profile publications; as such it may well have played a major part in his elevation to his current stature within the US political establishment. It may also, by the same token, have contributed substantially to President Bush's ability to strike a rapport on ethical matters with a sufficient proportion of the US electorate to facilitate his reelection in 2004, a result that many attributed largely to his ethical stance. It is a fact—perhaps a circular fact, but a fact nonetheless—that most people's gut feeling is that they should generally trust their gut feeling. To be told by an eminent professor that that's OK is probably rather comforting to most people, whether or not it actually should be.

Reflective equilibrium is, therefore, simply a method for discovering the moral status of actions.

Factoring Out the Cognitivism Question: Motivation and Means

The alert reader may have noticed that I devoted the last section to highlighting an example of a situation that exhibits precisely the problem I described in the previous section: a disconnect between the consensus of the relevant academic discipline and that of the general public. Specifically, professional ethicists are generally cognitivists whereas, whether they know it or not, the public are generally non-cognitivists. Kass has done himself big favours by abandoning the consensus of his field, but this disconnect means that from the point of view of engendering constructive debate he has done no one else any favours at all. Naturally I do not restrict my conclusion on this matter to the topic of human reproductive cloning: it extends to all issues on which the public exhibit a consensus deriving more from psychological pressures than from dispassionate logic, and in particular it extends to the desirability of defeating aging.

It is worth spelling out explicitly what this sort of situation means in practice. The natural, and strong, and indeed quite logical, tendency when arguing a particular ethical position is to start from precepts that one regards as so self-evident that one's interlocutor is sure to agree on them, and to work forwards in sufficiently deliberate steps that one can be optimistic that one's argument will be persuasive. Cognitivists generally view cognitivism as just such a precept—and therein lies the problem. An argument patently founded on the idea that the moral status of particular actions is objective, and thus on the (so I claim) inescapable corollary that one's gut feeling (e.g., repugnance) is not reliable at all, will inevitably wash over an unabashed non-cognitivist like water off a duck's back: the precept is rejected, so the entirety of what follows it is ignored. Critically, this is so whether or not the recipient of the cognitivist's argument has ever heard the word "cognitivism," because no training in philosophy is needed in order to understand that trust in one's own repugnance is a personal choice that conflicts with trust in dry ethical logic. This is, in my view, a fatal flaw in the rhetorical strategies employed by many pro-technology ethicists when discussing many issues, including extreme life extension.

Is there an alternative? I believe there is. It derives from a concept which has become associated with the noted ethicist John Rawls under the moniker "reflective equilibrium" (Rawls 1971). Rawls observed that a reasonable approach to determining whether something is morally unacceptable, acceptable or imperative is to develop *principles*—generalisations summarising what, *types* of things are unacceptable, acceptable or imperative—and to see whether those principles cover the case under consideration. In order to work optimally, however, one must revisit these principles in the light of any case of a situation in which other putatively trustworthy routes to an opinion on what is right and wrong (such as examination of one's repugnance) lead to conflicting conclusions. If only isolated situations exist in which one's intuition and one's stated principles conflict, the indicated way forward is to reject one's intuition in favour of the principles. If there are many such situations, on the other hand, one should seek a modified set of principles that better match one's intuition.

(From a scientific standpoint one can regard this as very similar to the principle of Occam's Razor in prioritising scientific hypotheses.) Reflective equilibrium is, therefore, simply a method for discovering the moral status of actions, and in this regard it is one of many alternatives, reliance on repugnance being another. What distinguishes it from other such methods—critically distinguishes it, I would contend—is its possession of two key characteristics:

- it is agnostic on the cognitivism/non-cognitivism issue;

- it seems to be the algorithm that modern societies, even if not necessarily most of their constituent individuals, actually execute in shifting their ethical positions over time.

I will not elaborate much further on the first of the above assertions. I merely note that the convergence of a set of moral precepts towards what one might call its "centre of moral gravity" is something that can happen whether or not the location of that centre is preordained by objective truth. Unlike the case of individual gut feelings about individual situations, it seems just as reasonable to suppose that the centre of gravity of an entire society's views on the entire universe of ethical issues is reliably in accordance with objective morality (which exists) as it is to suppose that that centre is arbitrarily located (and objective morality does not exist). Simply put, we would probably not be as happy as we are if *most* of us weren't already "right" about *most* moral issues. In other words, one can, I claim, be either a cognitivist or a non-cognitivist and still have no qualms about society's tendency to find its moral way using reflective equilibrium.

Reflective Equilibrium in Recent History

It may be valuable, on the other hand, to elaborate a little on my second assertion above—that modern societies actually use the reflective equilibrium algorithm as their main mechanism of moral exploration and progress.

There are many conspicuous issues regarding which contemporary Western society generally takes a different moral view than it did a century or two ago. Slavery, universal suffrage and homosexuality constitute a representative selection. In all these cases, the view that originally prevailed was overturned because the arguments for the status quo were eventually seen to come down to no more than a fear of the unknown, a faith in the "natural order" and other similarly unrooted emotions, whereas the arguments for change consisted of appeals to the incompatibility of the traditional position with agreed moral stances on matters that were claimed, and eventually agreed, to be inescapably equivalent (in moral terms) to the disputed one.

My efforts to hasten the defeat of aging must perforce incorporate not only direct, scientific, contributions ... but also contributions to the effort to bring society around to my way of thinking.

There may be a temptation to regard the success of reasoned arguments in these cases as supporting cognitivism, or at least as supporting the view that arguments that ethicists find appealing are likely also to be influential in the wider world. I dispute these conclusions. My interpretation is that these episodes are merely examples of reflective equilibrium in action, and thus, for reasons outlined above, say little about either the cognitivism/non-cognitivism question or the interest of the general public in what professional bioethicists think. The key point, I feel, is that the inescapability of an alleged equivalence between an issue on which the moral position is agreed and one on which it is initially disputed is not something that can be determined deductively: rather, it is a consequence of the acceptance of one or more principles (ethical generalisations, as described above) that encompass both issues. These principles, I claim, are not shown to be objectively true merely by their use in a successful reflective equilibrium process.

Cognitivism Agnostic Promotion of Indefinite Life Extension

This brings me to the crux of this essay. I take the view that the inexorable loss of vitality and rise in risk of death that we call "aging" is among—indeed, possibly foremost among—the sub-optimal features of life as we currently know it. Thus, I am necessarily keen to combat aging as much as possible as soon as possible. Since society in general does not share my fervour on this matter, and since the required technological advances will undoubtedly require very considerable investment of time and money, my efforts to hasten the defeat of aging must perforce incorporate not only direct, scientific, contributions to the development of that technology but also contributions to the effort to bring society around to my way of thinking, thereby causing these resources to be brought to bear (de Grey 2005a, 2005b). The considerations discussed above seem to me to give rise to a clear recommendation for the way forward on this matter, and it is one that does not always dominate the contemporary approaches of those commentators who already agree with me that aging is undesirable. It goes like this.

Since reflective equilibrium (a) often succeeds in changing people's minds and (b) is cognitivism-agnostic, we will benefit from constructing arguments that accelerate the reflective equilibrium process. We will benefit less, I feel, from arguments that purport to start from the objectivity of morality and thus from the unreliability of gut feelings, because such arguments fail at the outset with the many people who accept the wisdom of repugnance.

The difference between a cognitivism-agnostic argument and one starting from assertions of objective morality is subtle, which is doubtless why it seems to be easily overlooked. Essentially it comes down to the style of wording of introductory precepts. A line of reasoning that begins "As a starting-point, can we agree that X?" is cognitivism-agnostic, whereas one that begins "As a starting point, there is no doubt that X" is cognitivist. X is typically a moral position on a specific issue; the reflective equilibrium process then suggests a principle that "explains why" the agreed moral position is correct, and then that that principle also applies to the disputed issue. Typically either the principle, its applicability to the original agreed issue or its applicability to the disputed one are then challenged; third and subsequent issues then come into play. But the critical point is that at no stage in this process is the interlocutor's often deep-seated respect for his or her own gut feelings confronted head-on: rather, it is gradually and systematically undermined piece by piece. By this avoidance of a defensive reaction, success becomes, if not necessarily likely, at least possible.

The support of only a small (though preferably wealthy) minority of society is required to allow the relevant science to proceed as rapidly as it can.

Moral Acceptability Versus Moral Imperatives

In respect of combating aging, possibly the most important feature of a cognitivism-agnostic approach is that it lends itself quite readily to the conclusion that aging is not merely something we should let people combat if they wish but actually something that we all have a moral duty to help combat. The principles that one naturally brings to bear on this question when applying reflective equilibrium to it are ones supporting the moral equivalence of aging with phenomena that society has firmly decided that we do all have a duty to combat—most obviously, age-related diseases. It would be electorally unwise for a political party to campaign on a manifesto that committed it to abolishing public funding for research on cancer, diabetes and Alzheimer's disease and making commensurate tax cuts; this is because society overwhelmingly considers that expenditure on such research is a collective responsibility, not one that should be funded only by voluntary charitable donations. Arguments based on objective morality often lack this useful characteristic, because they tend to place more emphasis on speculations concerning what a post-aging world will be like, which are only as persuasive as the listener's inability to postulate contrary speculations permits.

This is not to say that "merely" persuading society that combating aging is morally acceptable is a failure, and that only the complete victory of persuading society that it is a moral imperative will do. Not only is the latter goal implausible in the short term, it is also unnecessary: in the first instance the support of only a small (though preferably wealthy) minority of society is required to allow the relevant science to proceed as rapidly as it can. As regards the rest of society, a muting of their opposition to such a goal is all that is needed. But this is a classic case of the "suitable outrageous extreme"—in any debate, one tends to have a much better chance of shifting one's interlocutor part-way towards one's own declared position than the whole way, irrespective of how far apart the two initial positions are. If, by arguing cogently that combating aging is a duty, we can convince quite a few active opponents (not least the theologians and bioethicists highlighted at the start of this essay) that it is at least an acceptable activity, we will have achieved much.

References

de Grey, A. D. N. J. 2003. The foreseeability of real anti-aging medicine: focusing the debate. *Experimental Gerontology* 38(9): 927-934.

de Grey, A. D. N. J. 2005a. Life extension, human rights, and the rational refinement of repugnance. *Journal of Medical Ethics* 31: 659-663.

de Grey, A. D. N. J. 2005b. Resistance to debate on how to postpone ageing is delaying progress and costing lives. *EMBO Reports* 6(S1): S49-S53.

Kass, L. R. 1971. Babies by means of in vitro fertilization: unethical experiments on the unborn? *New England Journal of Medicine* 285(21): 1174-1179.

Kass, L. R. 1997. The wisdom of repugnance. *The New Republic* 216(22): 17-26.

President's Council on Bioethics. 2003. *Beyond Therapy: Biotechnology and the Pursuit of Happiness.* http://www.bioethics.gov/reports/beyondtherapy/

Rawls, JB. 1971. *A Theory of Justice.* Cambridge, Massachusetts: Belknap Press of Harvard University Press.

9

Radical Life Extension Would Make People Less Human

Nicholas Agar

Nicholas Agar is a professor of ethics at the Victoria University of Wellington in New Zealand. He was elected as a Hastings Center Fellow in 2010.

The promise of radical life extension and other enhancements of the human condition come with a big trade-off. Many life extensionists are followers of a social movement known as transhumanism, the idea that it is both realistic and desirable to enhance human intellectual, physical, and psychological capacities beyond what is typically possible for humans. The trouble is, such "posthuman" radical enhancements could very well turn us into different beings and change the basic meaning of what it means to be human. Radical life extension could eliminate valuable experiences from human lives, and it is, in essence, a way of exiting the human species and becoming something else entirely. Radical enhancement will take humanity away from us.

Suppose someone makes you the following offer: They will boost your intellect to such an extent that your cognitive achievements far exceed those of Einstein, Picasso, Mozart, or any of our familiar exemplars of genius. You'll have a huge range of new experiences much more marvelous than climbing Mt. Everest, being present at full orchestra performances of Beethoven's Ninth Symphony, or consuming peyote. You'll

Nicholas Agar, "What Is Radical Enhancement?," *Humanity's End: Why We Should Reject Radical Enhancement,* Boston: MIT Press, 2010, pp. 1–15. Copyright © 2010 Massachusetts Institute of Technology, by permission of The MIT Press.

live for thousands of years. And the years you will gain won't have the diminished quality of those that modern medicine tends to provide. There'll be no need for oxygen bottles, Zimmer frames, bifocals, or any of the other standard accessories of extreme age in the early twenty-first century. The extra years will come with a guarantee of perfect health.

These are examples of what I will call *radical enhancement*. Radical enhancement involves improving significant human attributes and abilities to levels that greatly exceed what is currently possible for human beings. The radical enhancers who are [discussed here] propose to enhance intellects well beyond that of the genius physicist Albert Einstein, boost athletic prowess to levels that dramatically exceed that of the Jamaican sprint phenomenon Usain Bolt, and extend life spans well beyond the 122 years and 164 days achieved by the French super-centenarian Jeanne Calment.

Is Radical Enhancement Real?

Is the offer of radical enhancement one that should be taken seriously? If you received it by e-mail you might be tempted to file it in the folder reserved for unsolicited and ungrammatical offers of millions of dollars from the estates of people you've never met, and invitations to participate in multilevel marketing schemes. We will be exploring the ideas of a group of thinkers who make the offer in full earnestness. They propose to radically enhance our intellects and extend our life spans not by waving magic wands, but instead by administering a variety of technologies and therapies. These technologies and therapies are not available yet. But they could be soon. The writers of the *Star Trek* television series envisage our descendants two hundred years hence acquiring the ability to speedily travel to light-years-distant stars. If contemporary advocates of radical enhancement are right, then the individuals making those voyages will be more like the cerebral science officer Spock or the android Lieutenant Commander Data than the endearingly and annoyingly human Captain Kirk. It's also possible that we'll be alive to pilot the starships alongside them.

Fantastic offers tend to have catches, and radical enhancement is no exception to this rule.

Transhumanism Defined

Prominent among advocates of radical enhancement is a social movement known as *transhumanism*. Nick Bostrom, the movement's foremost philosopher, defines transhumanism as an "intellectual and cultural movement that affirms the possibility and desirability of fundamentally improving the human condition through applied reason, especially by developing and making widely available technologies to eliminate aging and to greatly enhance human intellectual, physical, and psychological capacities." Transhumanists do not have a monopoly on the idea of radical enhancement, however. Some would-be radical enhancers are far too busy working out how to boost intellects and extend lives to bother affiliating themselves with an Internet-based social movement.

Fantastic offers tend to have catches, and radical enhancement is no exception to this rule. I'll argue that there's another side to the vision of millennial life spans and monumental intellects. Radical enhancement threatens to turn us into fundamentally different kinds of beings, so different that we will no longer deserve to be called human. It will make us "posthuman." Although the benefits of radical enhancements of our minds and extensions of our lives may seem obvious—so obvious that they scarcely require defense—there is much that we stand to lose as we make the transition from human to posthuman. The aim of this [viewpoint] is to bring the costs of radical enhancement properly into focus. . . .

Eternal Life vs. Eternal Youth

Radical enhancement is not a new idea. Religion and myth are rich in accounts of humans seeking and undergoing radical enhancement. Those who transcribed myths or transmitted God's messages were alert to the possibility of a downside for such dramatic transformations. In ancient Greek myth, Zeus grants Tithonus the gift of eternal life. One thing he doesn't grant, however, is eternal *youth*. This leads, in some versions of the myth, to Tithonus' withering away to a cicada, a state in which (so the myth goes) he can be observed today. For Christians, the chief venue for radical enhancement is heaven. This is where the faithful experience an eternity of bliss in God's presence. According to many Christians, there's another, hotter location that offers a somewhat inferior version of eternal existence.

What's common to these stories is the view that one undergoes radical enhancement through the intercession of divine beings or by interacting with supernatural forces. The figures discussed [here] don't advocate prayer. They're offering DIY—do-it-yourself—radical enhancement. The idea that humans could be radically enhanced is not new; but the notion that it's something that we could arrange for ourselves certainly is. . . .

The right technologies can boost our mental powers and physical constitutions to levels far beyond those previously attained by humans.

Posthuman Capacity

Contemporary advocates of radical enhancement want to use a variety of technologies . . . [that] can serve our ideals about improvement rather than those of evolution. [Nick] Bostrom presents a concept of posthumanity that conceptually connects it with radical enhancement. He defines a posthuman as "a being that has at least one posthuman capacity," where a posthuman capacity is "a general central capacity greatly exceeding the maximum attainable by any current human being without recourse to new technological means." According to Bostrom, general central capacities include, but are not limited to, "health-span," which he understands as "the capacity to remain fully healthy, active, and productive, both mentally and physically"; cognition, which comprises intellectual capacities such as "memory, deductive and analogical reasoning, and attention, as well as special faculties such as the capacity to understand and appreciate music, humor, eroticism, narration, spirituality, mathematics"; and emotion, "the capacity to enjoy life and to respond with appropriate affect to life situations and other people." Bostrom thinks that the desirability of improving our central capacities is obvious. We all want to live longer, be healthier, reason better, and feel happier. The only surprise is that we may not have to content ourselves with the small improvements offered by better diets, exercise programs, and bridge lessons. The right technologies can boost our mental powers and physical constitutions to levels far beyond those previously attained by humans. . . .

A Dark Warning

I conjecture that the most dramatic means of enhancing our cognitive powers could in fact kill us; that the radical extension of our life spans could eliminate experiences of great value from our lives; and that a situation in which some humans are radically enhanced while others are not could lead to a tyranny of posthumans over humans.

What should we make of these darker forecasts? They're certainly logical possibilities—they describe futures that radical enhancement could create. But the same is true of the more optimistic outcomes favored by radical enhancement's advocates. How do we separate stories that demand serious attention from those that can be safely dismissed as science fiction? . . .

Some human values are likely to withstand, and even to be promoted by, radical enhancement. Longer lives and improved intellectual and physical prowess are certainly the objects of human desires; they aren't constructs of transhumanist ideology. The values that correspond with these human desires will doubtless survive our radical enhancement even if we exit the human species. My concern is for the violence done to other human values by the unchecked pursuit of extended lives and enlarged intellects.

Radical enhancement is a way of exiting the human species.

A Sci-Fi Example

For a science fiction example of how radical enhancement could preserve the biological bases of some human values while undermining the bases of others, consider the Cybermen, recidivist invaders of Earth in the BBC TV series *Doctor Who*. The Cybermen began existence as human beings. They . . . extended their life spans and boosted their intellectual and physical powers by replacing flesh with cybernetic implants. By the time the Doctor encounters them, all that remains of the humans they once were are biological brains completely encased by metal exoskeletons. . . .

It would be wrong to overstate the philosophical lessons that can be learned from this example; we shouldn't expect a nuanced analysis of the human condition and possible threats to it from a prime-time TV show. But the Cybermen can nevertheless serve as an illustration of how enhancement might promote certain human values at the expense of others. The self-modifications of the Cybermen are born out of the undeniably human desires to live longer and be smarter. They've achieved these ends, but only by suppressing other aspects of their humanity. For example, the Cybermen require inhibitors to prevent their human emotions from interfering with the directives of logic.

The Cybermen are creatures of fiction, and I won't be supposing that radical enhancement has effects anywhere as extreme as cyber-conversion, the process that turns humans into Cybermen. This [viewpoint] limits itself to the claim that radical enhancement is a way of exiting the human species that threatens many (but not all) of our valuable experiences. Experiences typical of the ways in which humans live and love are the particular focus of my species-relativism. I present these valuable experiences as consequences of the psychological commonalities that make humanity a single biological species. I argue that they are under threat from the manner and degree of enhancement advocated by [the life extensionists]. . . .

Many bioconservatives say that our humanity is the price we have to pay for radical enhancement. Some advocates of radical enhancement agree, effectively wishing our humanity goodbye and good riddance. But others think that we may undergo truly dramatic transformations without losing our humanity. . . .

I . . . argue that radical enhancement is indeed likely to take our humanity from us. The question we must then ask is what is lost along with our humanity.

10

The Personal, Social and Economic Case for Treating and Preventing Age Related Disease

Michael J. Rae et al.

The following viewpoint is written by Michael J. Rae and a group of other scientists and researchers in the fields of human aging, genetics, and ending age-related disease. Rae is a science writer for SENS Research Foundation, a nonprofit founded by biomedical gerontologist Aubrey de Grey, which works to develop, promote, and ensure access to rejuvenation biotechnologies that target the disabilities and diseases of aging. Rae is also a longtime member and former board member of the Calorie Restriction Society, a group that advocates and conducts research into calorie restriction as a way to slow the aging process.

The world is entering a period of unprecedented aging, with the number of late-life individuals expected to increase dramatically over the coming decades. Because the social and medical costs of population aging are so significant, the world must start preparing now for an impending global age crisis. Aggressive research is needed in order to develop interventions that can retard, arrest, and reverse aging damage. Failure to intervene in the aging process would have staggering social, financial, and humanitarian costs on a global scale. To preempt a global aging crisis, the au-

Michael J. Rae, et al., "The Demographic and Biomedical Case for Late-Life Interventions in Aging," *Science Translational Medicine*, vol. 2, no. 40, July 14, 2010, pp. 1–5. Copyright © 2010 by the American Association for the Advancement of Science. All rights reserved. Reproduced by permission.

thors advocate an ambitious global initiative to translate the findings of research on age-related diseases into interventions for aging humans "to retard, arrest, and even reverse aging damage, extending and even restoring the period of youthful health and functionality of older people." Extending the healthy lifespan would also have significant consequences, however, and this must be the subject of open public dialogue with the greater social good always being the goal.

The social and medical costs of the biological aging process are high and will rise rapidly in coming decades, creating an enormous challenge to societies worldwide. In recent decades, researchers have expanded their understanding of the underlying deleterious structural and physiological changes (aging damage) that underlie the progressive functional impairments, declining health, and rising mortality of aging humans and other organisms and have been able to intervene in the process in model organisms, even late in life. To preempt a global aging crisis, we advocate an ambitious global initiative to translate these findings into interventions for aging humans, using three complementary approaches to retard, arrest, and even reverse aging damage, extending and even restoring the period of youthful health and functionality of older people.

Age is the greatest risk factor for most major chronic diseases in the industrialized world and to an increasing degree in the developing world. After adolescent development, functionality declines progressively with age, and mortality rates increase exponentially, doubling roughly every 7 to 8 years after puberty. This exponentiality manifests as a progressive, roughly synchronous rise in the incidence of disease, disability, and death from chronic diseases beginning after midlife and suggests a causal—rather than a casual—relationship.

The physiological basis of these phenomena lies in the progressive lifelong accumulation of deleterious changes in the structure of the body at the molecular, cellular, and tissue levels. These changes (aging damage) arise primarily as damaging side effects of normal metabolism, aggravated by environmental toxins and unhealthy lifestyle. Aging damage contributes to pathology either directly (by impairing the function of specific biomolecules) or indirectly (by eliciting cellular or systemic responses that generally serve near-term protective functions but ultimately are deleterious). As damage accumulates, organisms suffer progressively diminished functionality, homeostasis, and plasticity, reducing the capacity to survive and recover from environmental challenge. These changes both contribute etiopathologically to specific age-related diseases and increase the organisms vulnerability to other insults that contribute to them, leading to increasing morbidity and mortality.

Surprise Conclusion

The surprising conclusion from the past two decades of research on biological aging is that aging is plastic: Within a species, maximum life span is not fixed but can be increased by dietary manipulation [particularly calorie restriction (CR)] or genetic manipulation [particularly dampened insulin/insulin-like growth factor-1 signaling (IIS)]. These interventions generally reduce the generation, enhance the repair, and/or increase the tolerance of the molecular and cellular damage of aging. Although our ability to assess "health span" in model organisms remains incomplete, these interventions generally preserve "youthful" functionality in regard to tested parameters and reduce the incidence of age-related disease.

There have long been calls for greater efforts to translate this research into clinical interventions to expand the healthy, productive period of human life. By targeting the aging damage that is responsible for the age-related rise in disease vulnerability, such interventions would reduce the incidence of most, if not all, age-related diseases in unison, by modulating the underlying biology that drives them all, rather than treating each in isolation, as in conventional medicine. To date, however, investments in such research by the National Institutes of Health (NIH) and its international equivalents have been disproportionately low relative to their potential return; for example, the NIH $28 billion budget allocates <0.1%— perhaps as little as $10 million—to research on biological aging. Contrast this allocation with the costs of medical care for today's aged, such as the current Medicare budget of $430 billion, and with projected outlays many times that number to treat future increases in the diseases of aging.

Intervention in the degenerative aging process need only lead to a simple delay in the appearance of age-related disability . . . in order to alleviate the projected social costs and challenge of global demographic aging.

Converging Trends

Calls for an intensive agenda or research on the biology of aging have particular salience today because of two converging trends: one demographic and one scientific. Demographically, we are entering a period of unprecedented global aging, as the ratio of retired elderly to younger workers increases dramatically within the next decades in both developing and industrialized nations. Age-related disease and disability greatly increase medical costs, even when adjusted for survivorship, and are major determinants of the decline in productivity and labor force participation after midlife. Thus, the results of biological aging are both a rise in social costs and a decrease in a national workforce's ability to produce the goods and services necessary to meet those costs. The costs of global aging to individuals and societies are therefore high and are projected to inflate into an unprecedented economic and social challenge in coming decades.

Effective Interventions

Scientifically, this phenomenon coincides with the first robust reports of effective interventions into the biological aging of mammals that are already in late middle age when treatment begins. In 2004, CR was first shown to extend life span in mice as old as 19 months, which is broadly equivalent to the current average age of postwar "baby boomers." And 2009 saw the first demonstration of pharmacological intervention into the biological aging of similar-aged mice, with preliminary evidence of delays in cancer incidence and other changes in gross pathology.

Intervention in the degenerative aging process need only lead to a simple delay in the appearance of age-related disability and rising medical costs in order to alleviate the projected social costs and challenge of global demographic aging. This alone would increase the ratio between productive workers of all ages and the dependent frail elderly, simultaneously expanding the resources available to bear the costs of supporting a subpopulation of frail elderly and reducing the relative size of that subpopulation during the critical period of demographic transition. The benefit to be gained from intervention in biological aging would be even greater, however, if it were able to not only delay the onset but reduce the absolute ultimate burden of age-related disease. . . .

In light of these convergent scientific and demographic phenomena, we advocate an intensive, dedicated, and focused R&D agenda by developed and rapidly developing nations globally, to devise interventions to restore and maintain the health and functionality of humans in late middle age and older.

Research Roadmap

Our consensus is that a realistic path toward this goal exists, by targeting age-associated changes that, based on existing research, are known or thought to be important primary components of human age-related degeneration and thus drivers of vulnerability to age-related disease. Here we outline such an agenda, focusing on targets that are likely to be biomedically tractable, even later in life, and would make efficient use of intellectual, capital, and temporal resources.

We propose a global biological aging research agenda focused on the detailed understanding of . . . overlapping core age changes and developing therapies for decelerating, arresting, and reversing them. . . .

Policy Priorities

Recognizing the potential of this research agenda to avert enormous economic, social, and human costs, we advocate that substantial new investments be made by governments, while engaging and facilitating the participation of the biomedical industry. A previous proposal that included one of us (R.N.B. [Robert N. Butler]) as an author suggested that the United States invest $3 billion annually (<1% of the current Medicare budget) in a broadly similar agenda; we suggest that this funding level is inadequate to deliver interventions in time to avert demographic crisis. We therefore urge a larger investment, targeted specifically to late-life interventions, matched by other developed and developing nations in proportion to the means and demographic urgency of each.

Because they would reverse existing age-related changes, the effects of regenerative therapies may be so rapid as to be amenable to direct testing for their effects on specific diseases in time frames similar to those of conventional medicines, allowing their evaluation in clinical trials within existing regulatory frameworks. However, new regulatory structures will also need to be developed for the unique features of this class of medicines, especially for interventions targeting modulation of the metabolic determinants of the rate of accumulation of aging damage, whose effects will be more global and will emerge more gradually. . . .

The Path Forward

We therefore advocate the development and implementation of all . . . intervention[s] in age-related degeneration discussed above, but with emphasis on metabolic and regenerative interventions, and on the most aggressive schedule possible, bearing in mind the urgency of the demographic challenge before us. We cannot be certain of success. Nor can the full range of social impacts, positive and negative, of a dramatic increase in healthy human life span be known with certainty in advance.

Recognizing the potential of this research agenda to avert enormous economic, social, and human costs, we advocate that substantial new investments be made by governments.

One obvious and quantifiable challenge that would result from a rapid decline in late-life mortality would be upward pressure on global population. Contrary to what is widely assumed, however, the net effect should be relatively minor. Because the effect on global population of adding each additional entire human life span (and one future parent) to the world is greater than the effect of adding some fraction of a life span onto each extant life, the effect of birth rates on population growth is much greater than the effect of late-life death rates. Without intervention in biological aging, the emerging global shift into sub-replacement fertility is likely to lead to the stabilization and later ongoing shrinkage of world population at ∼9 billion in the 2050–2070 range. . . .

The Need for Dialogue

This and other potential impacts of intervention in the degenerative aging process must be the subject of open, early, and serious public dialogue; in our view, such challenges should be met under the broad approach called the "vigilance principle": that action should be taken for the greater social good based on current knowledge, acknowledging uncertainty surrounding its possible future ramifications (positive and negative) and monitoring such consequences actively. The resilience and adaptability exhibited by human cultures throughout history should be recognized and engaged, with more specific policy-based remedies applied judiciously in cases in which organic social response proves insufficient to mitigate specific deleterious effects that actually (rather than hypothetically) emerge.

In the case of late-life intervention in human age-related degeneration, what we can be certain of today is that a policy of aging as usual will lead to enormous humanitarian, social, and financial costs. Efforts to avert that scenario are unequivocally merited, even if those efforts are costly and their success and full consequences uncertain. To realize any chance of success, the drive to tackle biological aging head-on must begin now.

Organizations to Contact

The editors have compiled the following list of organizations concerned with the issues debated in this book. The descriptions are derived from materials provided by the organizations. All have publications or information available for interested readers. The list was compiled on the date of publication of the present volume; the information provided here may change. Be aware that many organizations take several weeks or longer to respond to inquiries, so allow as much time as possible.

AARP
601 E St. NW, Washington, DC   20049
(888) 687-2277
e-mail: member@aarp.org
website: www.aarp.org

AARP, formerly known as the American Association of Retired Persons, is a nonpartisan organization that seeks to improve the aging experience for all Americans. It is committed to the preservation of Social Security and Medicare. AARP publishes the magazine *Modern Maturity* and the newsletter *AARP Bulletin*. Issue statements and congressional testimony can be found at its website.

Alliance for Aging Research
750 17th St. NW, Suite 1100, Washington, DC   20006
(202) 293-2856 • fax: (202) 955-8394
e-mail: info@agingresearch.org
website: www.agingresearch.org

The Alliance for Aging Research is a nonprofit organization that works to accelerate the pace of medical discoveries to maximize healthy aging, independence, and quality of life for older Americans. The organization publishes a monthly e-mail newsletter and its website includes a wide array of articles, research, and updates for those interested in life extension topics.

American Geriatrics Society (AGS)
40 Fulton St., 18th Floor, New York, NY   10038
(212) 308-1414 • fax: (212) 832-8646
e-mail: info.amger@americangeriatrics.org
website: www.americangeriatrics.org

The American Geriatrics Society (AGS) is a professional organization of health-care providers that aims to improve the
health and wellbeing of older adults. AGS helps shape attitudes, policies, and practices regarding health care for older
people. The Society's publications include the book *The American Geriatrics Society's Complete Guide to Aging and Health*,
the magazines *Journal of the American Geriatrics Society* and
Annals of Long-Term Care: Clinical Care and Aging, and *The
AGS Newsletter*.

American Society on Aging (ASA)
71 Stevenson St., Suite 1450, San Francisco, CA   94105-2938
(415) 974-9600 • fax: (415) 974-0300
e-mail: info@asaging.org
website: www.asaging.org

The American Society on Aging (ASA) is an organization of
health-care and social service professionals, researchers, educa-
tors, businesspersons, senior citizens, and policymakers that is
concerned with all aspects of aging and works to enhance the
wellbeing of older individuals. Its publications include the bi-
monthly newspaper *Aging Today* and the quarterly journal
Generations.

Fight Aging!
e-mail: reason@fightaging.org
website: www.fightaging.org

Fight Aging! began in 2004 as part of the nonprofit advocacy
group the Longevity Meme and has since evolved into an en-
tity in its own right. The mission of Fight Aging! is to encourage the development of medical technologies, lifestyles, and
other means that will help people live comfortably, healthily,

and capably for as long as they desire, well beyond the current limits of mortality. The Fight Aging! website includes articles on longevity activism and advocacy, medical and scientific developments, and healthy living for older adults. Fight Aging! publishes a weekly e-mail newsletter that features commentary, news, and opinion pieces on healthy life extension topics, as well. Back issues are archived online, and the organization also publishes a daily blog on the site.

Future of Humanity Institute
Faculty of Philosophy, University of Oxford, Suite 8
Littlegate House 16/17 St Ebbe's St., Oxford OX1 1PT
+44(0)1865 286279 · fax: +44(0)1865 286983
e-mail: fhi@philosophy.ox.ac.uk
website: www.fhi.ox.ac.uk

The Future of Humanity Institute is a multidisciplinary research institute at the University of Oxford in England. The Institute's work centers on how anticipated technological developments may affect the human condition in fundamental ways—and how humans can better understand, evaluate, and respond to radical change. The Institute publishes an informative monthly newsletter, and its website publishes the daily blog *Overcoming Bias*. The site also features research papers funded by the Institute as well as other readings on the ethics and consequences of life enhancement and life extension.

Institute for Ethics and Emerging Technologies (IEET)
Williams 119, Trinity College, 300 Summit St.
Hartford, CT 06106
(860) 297-2376
e-mail: director@ieet.org
website: www.ieet.org

The Institute for Ethics and Emerging Technologies (IEET) is a nonprofit founded by philosopher Nick Bostrom and bioethicist James Hughes. IEET advocates for a responsible, constructive approach to emerging human enhancement technologies, encourages public policies for their safe and equitable use, and works to cultivate academic, professional and popular appreciation about their impacts. In addition to offering a variety of pro-longevity articles and research on its website, IEET publishes a series of white papers by notable names in the field, a weekly newsletter, frequent podcasts, and a daily blog.

International Federation on Ageing (IFA)

351 Christie St., Toronto, Ontario
  M6G 3C3
  Canada
+1 416 342-1655 • fax: +1 416 392-4157
e-mail: atam@ifa-fiv.org
website: www.ifa-fiv.org

The International Federation on Ageing (IFA), a nongovernmental organization (NGO) with a membership base of NGOs, the corporate sector, academia, government, and individuals, believes in "generating positive change for older people throughout the world by stimulating, collecting, analyzing, and disseminating information on rights, policies, and practices that improve the quality of life of people as they age." It publishes the quarterly journal, *Ageing International*, and a monthly newsletter for its members, *Intercom*.

LifeStar Institute

7512 Dr. Phillips Dr., Suite 50-924, Orlando, FL   32819
(407) 462-4294
e-mail: main@LifeStarInstitute.org
website: www.lifestarinstitute.org

The LifeStar Institute is a nonprofit "dedicated to averting the pending global aging crisis in the pursuit of personnel, sciences, and processes to develop therapies that restore knowledge and productivity." The organization's website offers a wide variety of publications on aging topics, including "Why Population Aging Matters—A Global Perspective," from the National Institute on Aging, and "The Economic Burden of

Chronic Disease on the United States," by The Milken Institute, in addition to its own writings. The organization also publishes an occasionally updated blog on its website.

Methuselah Foundation

8021 Flint St., Springfield, VA   22153
(703) 440-5141 • fax: (703) 229-6339
e-mail: info@mfoundation.org
website: www.methuselahfoundation.org

Founded by radical life extension scientist Aubrey de Grey, the Methuselah Foundation is a nonprofit working to find a cure for age-related disease. The organization funds the Methuselah Mouse Prize (Mprize), a multi-million dollar competitive research prize for the successful extension of healthy lifespan in the laboratory mouse. The group's website offers a wide variety of scientific articles and research papers concerning radical life extension and the biomedical advances that seek to make it a reality. The site publishes a daily Methuselah Foundation blog and provides numerous links to other pro-longevity blogs and online resources.

National Council on Aging (NCOA)

1901 L St. NW, 4th Floor, Washington, DC   20036
(202) 479-1200
e-mail: info@ncoa.org
website: www.ncoa.org

The National Council on Aging (NCOA) is a nonprofit service and advocacy organization acting as a national voice for older Americans and the community organizations that serve them. NCOA brings together nonprofit organizations, businesses, and government to help improve the lives of older adults, working to help seniors find jobs and benefits, improve their health, live independently, and remain active in their communities. NCOA's quarterly magazine, *Journal of the National Council on the Aging*, provides tools and insights for community service organizations.

National Institute on Aging (NIA)
31 Center Dr., MSC 2292, Bethesda, MD   20892
(800) 222-2225
e-mail: niaic@nia.nih.gov
website: www.nia.nih.gov

The National Institute on Aging (NIA) is one of the twenty-seven institutes and centers of the federal government's National Institutes of Health. It leads a broad scientific effort to understand the nature of aging and to extend the healthy, active years of life. NIA's Division of Aging Biology promotes and supports research and training on the physical mechanisms that underlie normal aging and age-related diseases and decline. The NIA's Division of Geriatrics and Clinical Gerontology supports research on health and disease in the aged and research on aging over the human lifespan. The NIA website offers information about all of the organization's various research programs, as well as fact sheets and reports on aging and life extension topics.

Presidential Commission for the Study of Bioethical Issues
1425 New York Ave. NW, Suite C100, Washington, DC   20005
(202) 233-3960 • fax: (202) 233-3990
e-mail: info@bioethics.gov
website: www.bioethics.gov

The Presidential Commission for the Study of Bioethical Issues is an advisory panel of the nation's leaders in medicine, science, ethics, religion, law, and engineering. The Commission advises the US president on bioethical issues arising from advances in biomedicine and related areas of science and technology. The Commission seeks to identify and promote policies and practices that ensure that scientific research, healthcare delivery, and technological innovation are conducted in a socially and ethically responsible manner. The Commission conducts research into a wide array of biomedical issues, including age retardation, life enhancement, and life extension. Reports on these topics are archived on the Commission's website and include the 2010 paper, "New Directions: The Ethics of Synthetic Biology and Emerging Technologies."

SENS Research Foundation
110 Pioneer Way, Suite J, Mountain View, CA   94041
(650) 938-6100
website: www.sens.org

Founded in March 2009 by biomedical gerontologist and radical life extension proponent Aubrey de Grey, the SENS Research Foundation is a nonprofit that works to develop, promote, and ensure access to rejuvenation biotechnologies that target the disabilities and diseases of aging. SENS is an acronym for "Strategies for Engineered Negligible Senescence," which the group defines as an integrated set of medical techniques designed to restore youthful molecular and cellular structure to aged tissues and organs. The SENS Research Foundation website offers a variety of technical papers regarding such topics, as well as general information about the group's mission and activities.

Bibliography

Books

Aubrey de Grey and Michael Rae	*Ending Aging: The Rejuvenation Breakthroughs That Could Reverse Human Aging in Our Lifetime.* New York: St. Martins Press, 2007.
David Ewing Duncan	*When I'm 164: The New Science of Radical Life Extension, and What Happens If It Succeeds.* New York: TED Books, 2012.
Gregory Fahy et al., eds.	*The Future of Aging: Pathways to Human Life Extension.* New York: Springer, 2010.
James Golczewski	*Life Extension: Current and Future Possibilities.* Camp Hill, PA: Sunbury Press, 2012.
Stephen Hall	*Merchants of Immortality: Chasing the Dream of Human Life Extension.* New York: Mariner Books, 2004.
Leon Kass	*Ageless Bodies: Beyond Therapy—A Report of the President's Council on Bioethics.* Washington, DC: PCBE, 2003.
Raymond Kurzweil and Terry Grossman	*Fantastic Voyage: The Science Behind Radical Life Extension.* New York: Rodale, 2004.
Derek Maher and Calvin Mercer, eds.	*Religion and the Implications of Radical Life Extension.* New York: Palgrave Macmillan, 2009.

Thomas Mooney *Live Forever or Die Trying: The History and Politics of Life Extension.* Bloomington, IN: Xlibris, 2011.

James Schultz and Robert Binstock *Aging Nation: The Economics and Politics of Growing Older in America.* Westport, CT: Praeger, 2006.

Jonathan Weiner *Long for This World: The Strange Science of Immortality.* New York: Ecco, 2010.

Arlene Weintraub *Selling the Fountain of Youth: How the Anti-Aging Industry Made a Disease Out of Getting Old—And Made Billions.* New York: Basic Books, 2010.

Periodicals and Internet Sources

Nick Bostrom "Recent Developments in the Ethics, Science, and Politics of Life-Extension," *Aging Horizons*, vol. 3, Autumn/Winter 2005.

Adam Bulger "Want to Live Forever? The Human-Life-Extension Movement Sees a Glorious Future for Us All," *Hartford Advocate*, August 8, 2008.

John Davis "Collective Suttee: Is It Just to Develop Life Extension if It Will Not Be Possible to Provide It to Everyone?," *Annals NY Academy of Sciences*, vol. 1019, June 2004.

John Davis   "The Prolongevists Speak Up: The Life-Extension Ethics Session at the 10th Annual Congress of the International Association of Biomedical Gerontology, 2004," *The American Journal of Bioethics*, vol. 4, no. 4, December 2004.

Julian Dibbell   "The Fast Supper," *New York Magazine*, October 23, 2006.

Lydia Dugdale and Autumn Alcott Ridenour   "Making Sense of the Roman Catholic Directive to Extend Life Indefinitely," *Hastings Center Report*, vol. 41, no. 2, 2011.

Jennifer Fishman, Robert Binstock, and Marcie Lambrix   "Anti-Aging Science: The Emergence, Maintenance, and Enhancement of a Discipline," *Journal of Aging Studies*, vol. 22, no. 4, December 2008.

Lev Grossman   "2045: The Year Man Becomes Immortal," *Time*, February 10, 2011.

Robin Holliday   "The Extreme Arrogance of Anti-Aging Medicine," *Biogerontology*, vol. 10, no. 2, April 2009.

Alison Kadlec et al.   "The Science of Aging Gracefully: Scientists and the Public Talk About Aging Research," Public Agenda, 2005. www.publicagenda.org.

Steven Leckart   "How Beer, Oprah and Sergey Brin Can Help Cure Aging," *Wired*, October 19, 2010. www.wired.com.

Carl Marziali — "Reaching Toward the Fountain of Youth," *Trojan Family Magazine*, December 7, 2010. http://uscnews.usc.edu.

Michael Mason — "One for the Ages: A Prescription That May Extend Life," *New York Times*, October 31, 2006.

Sherwin Nuland — "Do You Want to Live Forever?," *MIT Technology Review*, February 2005.

S. Jay Olshansky — "A Wrinkle in Time—A Modest Proposal to Slow Aging and Extend Healthy Life," *Slate*, November 12, 2010. www.slate.com.

S. Jay Olshansky et al. — "In Pursuit of the Longevity Dividend: What Should We Be Doing to Prepare for the Unprecedented Aging of Humanity?," *The Scientist*, vol. 20, March 2006. www.grg.org.

Caspar Llewellyn Smith — "Aubrey de Grey: We Don't Have to Get Sick as We Get Older," *The Observer*, July 31, 2010.

Gregory Stock, Daniel Callahan, and Aubrey de Grey — "The Ethics of Life Extension," *Rejuvenation Research*, vol. 10, no. 3, September 1, 2007.

Rebecca Traister — "Diet Your Way to a Long, Miserable Life!," *Salon*, November 22, 2006. www.salon.com.

Nicholas Wade — "Quest for a Long Life Gains Scientific Respect," *New York Times*, September 28, 2009.

Index

CPSIA information can be obtained at www.ICGtesting.com
Printed in the USA
LVOW12n1131100813

347152LV00002B/2/P